This book is both thought-provoking and deeply moving, offering a fresh perspective on what it means to place children genuinely at the centre of our decisions. With an exceptional blend of insight and heart, it invites readers to reflect, to reimagine, and to act—making it as relevant to families as it is to educators and leaders, and as inspiring as it is practical.

Andrea Garcia Herrera | Marketing professional, Montessori Lead Educator and Coach

Led By The Child is a warm and engaging celebration of the work and thinking of Maria Montessori. There is an honest style in the writing that enables Karen Chetwynd to tackle some of the questions and challenges made to, and of, the modern concept of Montessori education, providing an account of Montessori education that is realistic in terms of what modern life, and modern education systems, have to throw at us. There is a reminder of what Montessori has offered education in terms of understanding children and their learning, alongside recognising that educators, parents and children are all in it together when we tackle the modern world and navigate our way through it. Karen draws out the relevancy of Montessori's ideas for the modern day, while challenging the stereotype that it is just for the elite few. There are thought provoking questions around what is education for, with real world examples, but overall a strong sense of advocacy for children and their learning.

Professor Verity Campbell Barr | Director of Plymouth Institute of Education, Plymouth Institute of Education (Faculty of Arts, Humanities and Business)

What stood out most to me in *Led By The Child* was Karen's call to center children not just as learners—but as leaders. As someone working at the intersection of AI, learner autonomy, and community-driven education through organizations, I found this book both affirming and deeply expansive. In Chapter 3, she writes:

'We cannot design for the child—we must design with the child.'

'Children are not voiceless. They are unheard.'

That shift—from compliance to co-creation—is exactly what's needed in today's learning systems. Karen makes a powerful case that Montessori's core principles aren't just for classrooms—they're for everyone. She reframes Montessori as a tool for human development, rooted not in privilege, but in history: refugee camps, mental hospitals, slums. This isn't soft pedagogy—it's a radical, scalable model for equity. I also appreciated how she tackled the tension between values-driven education and metrics. In a numbers-driven world, her reminder that "what gets measured gets valued" is important—but so is her call to rethink what success even looks like. Thank you for bringing such clarity, vision, and groundedness to the future of education

Marina A. Solovyov | Education Director at Ludwitt, Austin, Texas

Karen Chetwynd's *Led By The Child* is not so much a book as it is a quietly radical manifesto, though one wrapped in a voice so calm, measured, and professionally poised that you almost miss the revolutionary undertones. Almost.

From the outset, Chetwynd dismantles the convenient fiction that education is something adults "do" to children. She replaces it with a bracingly clear proposition: the child is already doing the work of becoming; our job is not to obstruct. This is Montessori stripped of boutique trappings and repositioned as a social equaliser, less mahogany learning tower, more kitchen table with two pineapples and a stopwatch.

Her dry wit surfaces in unexpected places, likening teachers to farmers who tend this year's crop without sentimental illusion, or comparing schools to biscuit factories churning out uniform outcomes. These moments disarm the reader just enough to let the deeper truths land: capability, not compliance, is the goal.

What elevates the work beyond educational theory is Chetwynd's strategic mind at play. She moves from philosophical foundations to operational imperatives, teacher training, parental engagement, and community partnerships, without losing sight of the central premise: the child leads, we follow with intent.

In a sector awash with platitudes, *Led By The Child* is that rare, necessary thing: visionary without vanity, practical without pedantry, and quietly, utterly subversive.
Sarah Tucker | Novelist, Broadcaster, and Biographer of Edward de Bono's biography *Love Laterally*, and www.theboardroom.bard

What struck me most is Karen's honesty about the limits of current research (Chapter 3), and her urgent call to shift from ritual to principle-based practice. *Led By The Child* offers a rare blend of analytical depth and soul-driven advocacy.
Hans Lagerweij | CEO, Flying Dutchman Consultancy | Board Advisor & Director | Author of *The Why Whisperer: How to Motivate and Align Teams That Get Your Strategy Done*

Finally, a book that bridges traditional schooling with child-led learning. Karen speaks with authority and empathy—every chapter gives you a tool you can use today.
Kumar R. Parakala | Chairman, Thriveco, USA Today Bestselling Author, Amazon Bestselling Author and International Impact Award Winner

Led By The Child is a passionate call to transform global education by putting children's voices at the heart of learning—offering practical strategies, inspiring stories, and a compelling case for making Montessori inclusive, adaptable, and accessible to all.
Tamara Nall | CEO & Founder, The Leading Niche

Led By The Child is a thoughtful and visionary call to reimagine education as a partnership, one that honors the unique potential of each child and the essential role of the family. Karen Chetwynd challenges outdated models and invites us to consider what's possible when curiosity, dignity, and purposeful learning are placed at the center. While not every context will adopt the Montessori method fully, this book offers principles that can strengthen any educational setting.
Carl Grant III | Author, *How to Live the Abundant Life*

Led By The Child

Unlocking the Power of Montessori for All

BY KAREN CHETWYND
CEO, Montessori Global Education

[Montessori St Nicholas Ltd &
St. Nicholas Montessori Training Ltd (MCI)]

Copyright © 2025 Karen Chetwynd
Published in United Kingdom
www.montessori-globaleducation.org

All rights reserved. No part of this book may be reproduced or transmitted in any form or by any means, electronic or mechanical, including photocopying, recording, or by an information storage and retrieval system – except by a reviewer who may quote brief passages in a review to be printed in a magazine or newspaper – without permission in writing from the copyright holder.

All trademarks, service marks, trade names, product names, and logos appearing in this publication are the property of their respective owners.

ISBN (ebook) 978-1-9191831-0-7
ISBN (pbk) 978-1-9191831-1-4
ISBN (hcv) 978-1-9191831-2-1

Contents

Dedication 11

Acknowledgements 13

Foreword 15

Introduction 19

Part 1: Make Montessori Available Everywhere 29

Chapter 1: The Problem 31
    Why Isn't Montessori Available Worldwide? 31
    Montessori Today 37

Chapter 2: The Solution 49
    What Is Child-Centered Learning? 49
    Montessori for All—Accessibility and Perception 52
    Adapting to Survive 53
    Refocus the Lens—Our Pillars in Practice 56
    Our Future 61

Part 2: Demonstrate, Convincingly, the Impact Montessori Can Have on Every Child 63

Chapter 3: The Problem 65
    Why Isn't Montessori's Impact Understood? 65
    Philosophy & Pedagogy: Security, Time & Effort 70
    Authentic versus Sustainable 73
    When Disaster Hits, It Hits Children Hardest 77
    Limited Research 80

Chapter 4: The Solution 83
    We Champion Principles over Ritual 83
    We Set Priorities, Teaching the Most Necessary Skills 90
    We Deal with Challenging Situations 92
    We Celebrate Journeys of Self-Discovery 95
    We Seek Youth Advocates 97

Part 3: Build Montessori Skills 99

Chapter 5: The Problem 101
    Why Aren't Children Heard? 101
    The Challenge of Diversity 107
    If We Don't Listen, We Can't Accommodate Diverse Views 112
    Standardized Evaluation Is Possible Only When All
    Parties Agree 119
    Co-creation 121

Chapter 6: The Solution 125
    Advisory Panels and Evaluation Processes 125
    Engagement and Encouragement in
    Co-creation 128

**Part 4: Make Children Visible and Their Voices Vital
in Their Education** 135

Chapter 7: The Problem 137
    Why Are Stakeholders at Odds? 137
    The Pitch and the Plans 141
    Cultural Expectations / Societal Norms 143
    Assessment Outcomes Focused on "Recognized"
    Successes 149
    The Art of Observation 150
    The Bottom Line 154

Chapter 8: The Solution 157
    Promote Learner Voices & Elevate Recognition 158
    Refocus on Detailed Research 160
    Promote Observation/Mentoring Among Educators 164

Conclusion: Montessori's Future as an Accessible, Inclusive Model for All 169
    Our Goal 170
    Home-Start: A Montessori Success Story 172
    A Closer Look 174
    Changing Attitudes 176
    Volunteer Prime 178
    Calls to Action 183

About the Author 185

Dedication

To my children, Logan and Esme, who teach me everything every day.
To my mum, my original "Montessori-inspired" first educator.

Acknowledgements

Special thanks to my writing coach and mentor, Phoenix Roberts, without whom this book could not have been completed.

Thank you to my husband and my dad for their encouragement every day.

Thanks also to Preeti Patel, Beatrice Luca, Andrea Garcia Herrera, Sinéad King, Jo McIntyre, Michelle Rice, Rachel Shorter, Yelena Levashina, and Millie James—we are making a difference; your commitment and dedication mean the world to our work and our team.

To Geeta Sidhu-Robb for her encouragement and challenge, for supporting my development, resilience, and determination to lead confidently and conscientiously. Your observations will continue to have a lasting impact. Thank you.

Foreword

As the former Chair of Montessori Global's Board of Trustees, I am honored to write the foreword for this book.

In fact, it is with deep purpose and pride that we present this book, not as a manifesto for an educational alternative, but as a timely reminder that Montessori is not merely a method. It is a philosophy. A tried, tested, and transformational way of seeing the child, the adult, and the society they are both shaping.

Montessori is for everyone. And yet, for far too long, it has not been available to everyone.

This work begins with the belief that Montessori education—holistic, human-centered, and profoundly respectful—is not a privilege. It is a right. In the face of global inequality, fractured schooling systems, and generations of families for whom education has been more exclusionary than empowering, we see an urgent need to make Montessori visible, accessible, and confidently situated in every context where children grow and communities strive.

This book issues a clear call:

1. Make Montessori available everywhere.
2. Demonstrate, convincingly, its impact on every child.
3. Build Montessori skills in parents, educators, and children alike.
4. And most importantly, make children visible—and their voices vital—in their own education.

That last point is the cornerstone. A child who is seen and heard becomes an active participant in their own becoming. A two-year-old, stamping her foot and declaring, "I'm independent!" isn't misbehaving—she is becoming. She is claiming space in the world, not for rebellion but for agency. That sense of autonomy, nurtured instead of suppressed, is the beginning of responsible adulthood. It is also the soul of Montessori.

Historically, schools have functioned more like factories than communities. Children have been viewed through the lens of efficiency and output, expected to conform to externally imposed benchmarks. If they failed to meet the system's expectations, the assumption was that the child failed, not the system.

Montessori shifts that perspective entirely.

To honor each child's dignity, we must first accept that education is not something done to children; it is their lived experience, day by day, in the present. The Montessori classroom—whether in a school, a home, a community center, or a parent's lap—is a living environment of observation, preparation, and trust. It centers the child not by removing adult guidance, but by redefining what true guidance looks like. Montessori adults—parents, teachers, caregivers—serve as stewards, not controllers. The goal is not compliance. It is a capability.

Of course, this shift is uncomfortable for some. In the traditional system, adults are taught to seek control over outcomes, curriculum, and over children's attention and behavior. Montessori asks us instead to cultivate responsibility, in ourselves and in the child. That takes courage. It takes humility. In many under-served and under-resourced communities, it takes rebuilding trust because education has often failed those communities.

Montessori is not a model of perfection. It is a practice of presence. And when it is placed in the hands of people who live with purpose, it thrives, even, and perhaps especially, in places where standardized education has faltered. In these contexts, Montessori is not only relevant. It is revolutionary.

This book does not claim to hold all the answers. It offers something more essential: possibility. It presents real-world examples, practical suggestions, and visionary insight into what becomes possible when we allow Montessori to be ordinary, woven into the fabric of everyday life—a parent in a market teaching math through carrots and pineapples. A teacher finding the courage to pause a lesson for a moment of movement or quiet. Children solving problems not because they were told to, but because they want to.

Montessori thrives in these moments. And those moments, when multiplied across households, classrooms, and cultures, begin to change the world.

We are proud to support the expansion of this movement through work in schools located in communities that are too often overlooked. In places where challenge is the norm and resources are scarce, we are helping develop Montessori teacher training, parent education, and sustainable systems of care, not as charity, but as a partnership. Because every child deserves to be seen, every community deserves to be served.

Montessori belongs to all of us, not just those who can afford it or access it. It is a philosophy that calls us to be more human in our approach to raising humans. It begins not with sweeping reform but with simple changes in how we see, hear, and hold the child.

This is our invitation: to see Montessori as a support mechanism for life, not school; to hear children not as noise, but as vital contributors to their own learning; and to embrace this approach not as new, but as timeless.

Education is not a preparation for life. As Dewey reminded us, it is life itself.

Let us live it well.

Geeta Sidhu-Robb

Introduction

> *This is education, understood as a help to life; an education from birth, which feeds a peaceful revolution and unites all in a common aim, attracting them as to a single center. Mothers, fathers, politicians: all must combine in their respect and help for this delicate work of formation, which the little child carries on in the depth of a profound psychological mystery, under the tutelage of an inner guide. This is the bright new hope for mankind.*
> —Maria Montessori[1]

When I became Chief Executive Officer of Montessori Global Education in June of 2024, I felt a need to redefine how the world sees the Montessori Method. We're perceived by some as **elitist**, but I maintain that Dr. Montessori's child-centered philosophy can be a positive force in **every** child's education. From the day a baby is born, parents can prepare the child for a life of curiosity, reasoning, and growth. Montessori is here to help by giving children the tools they need to thrive. Parents light the fire within their children. Montessori stands with them to help fan that tiny flame into a burning desire to continue learning throughout their lives.

Long before they enter a "school system," children are learning. Maria Montessori wanted those early years to be understood and recognized; to be the cornerstone of success for life. Montessori assists parents in helping their children develop love for learning, critical thinking, and an expansive view of the world, skills that give those children tremendous advantages throughout life. Within formal learning, or "school" systems, Montessori promotes and supports a

---

[1] Maria Montessori, *The Absorbent Mind*. Adyar, Madras, India: Theosophical Publishing House, 1949.

quality education for every student at every level, in full cooperation with existing curricula. Outside of formal education, we encourage continual learning to enhance one's occupation, community projects, hobbies, or simply for personal pleasure, enriching our lives in ways too numerous to describe.

Our Vision

As I look 10 or 20 years down the road, what do I hope to see?

A world where the power of Montessori education is available to everyone.

This vision developed as I realized that the Montessori Method needs to be presented and encouraged as a model of leveling access for all learners. While school systems are unequal (the natural state of organizations that serve a broad community), opportunities provided by educators don't need to be. We must seek ways to encourage teachers to be confident in facilitating opportunities for discovery and exploration suited to each child. The potential impact is as yet intangible for us as an organization. As we seek greater opportunities for students, we seek better measurements of student growth and the effectiveness of our Method. We recognize that the world has changed since Dr. Montessori set out to improve education, that her best work won't always be the most effective for our generation's needs, and that whatever developments we make will be foundation stones on which our successors will further review the Method.

Montessori has a century-long history of service to education, mostly through special, private Montessori Schools. These are wonderful facilities that do great work for their students, but what about areas where there are no Montessori schools? Can we do nothing for them? Where they do exist, can we expand the connection to communities and show the value we have outside those specialized facilities? We can and, if we're to fulfill Maria Montessori's original purpose, we have an obligation to do so.

Our Mission

To fulfil our obligations in the 21st Century, I see a need to:

> *1) Make Montessori available everywhere.*
> *2) Demonstrate, convincingly, the impact Montessori can have on every child.*
> *3) Build Montessori skills among parents, children, and educators.*
> *4) Make children visible and their voices vital in their education.*

On that last point, which is the cornerstone of our philosophy, my two-year-old hit it on the head recently. While stamping her foot about something, she declared—forcefully—"I'm independent!"

A half-century ago, she wouldn't have been. Schools were like cookie factories, churning out millions of chocolate chip or oatmeal raisin cookies each day. Each school's curriculum and method were standardized and imposed on every student, and students were expected to meet school standards. When they didn't, it was assumed the student had failed, not the school. Sadly, some schools still operate this way.

Today, we understand that children have individual needs that education factories can't meet. Giving up the simplicity of the regimented, in-the-box educational model means giving up some control over the student. There is resistance to this paradigm. People are asking, "Who, then, should control a child's education?"

First, parents are the legal guardians of their children. It's their right and obligation to oversee everything that concerns those children.

They should have the most power in education decisions because, with a few rare exceptions, they always have the best interests of their child at heart. Good teachers love their students, but teachers are like farmers in one respect: Next year, we will see a whole new crop in the field. The parental commitment is forever.

Second, teachers need to maintain control over their classrooms, but not over individual students. Chaos makes for a poor learning environment, but swinging the pendulum to the other end of its spectrum is equally unproductive. As I write this, we're working on several projects where school officials have identified a range of significant challenges for their student population, and yet they remain committed to offering a Montessori educational experience. We are proud to be co-creating teacher training provision within these schools to ensure the application of the Montessori method is sustainable for many generations to come. We are committed to supporting an evolving model of self-growth, development of community connection, and wider training for families and their local communities. But these are isolated, under-served, in areas of deprivation—a location for an educational experience that, traditionally, has not had a great reputation—where problems are more likely avoided or worsened than solved. Those issues are individual to each child. Our challenge lies in going into any school and getting people unfamiliar with our methods to adopt a Montessori ethos. They fear losing the control they have over their classrooms. It's not about that; it's about redefining control to find that balance which produces the best results for each child.

Finally, children have, traditionally, been ignored in this discussion; however, children who feel a sense of control over their educational experience feel greater enthusiasm for and interest in learning. The global homeschool movement has long since validated this hypothesis. If we can get students in a situation where they feel like they have some control, their natural exuberance and energy can be channeled in the right direction. They'll be making life decisions someday—and that someday is approaching faster than any of us would like to admit.

Parents and teachers should want children to stand up for things they believe in and to believe in things that make the world a better place. We need them to become capable, autonomous beings who can make it on their own if they are to fulfill that goal.

> *Education is not a preparation for life; education is life itself.*
> —John Dewey[2]

Hearing children is only half of my fourth mission point. The other half is visibility. We shouldn't look into a classroom of 10 or 20 or 30 and see *a class*. We should see 10, 20 or 30 **students**. Most of them started showing their personalities within weeks of birth, some within minutes! If we forget that each is a unique human being, they lose some of their humanity in our view. How can we serve them best if we don't see them as who and what they truly are?

The Problem

In a word, *irresponsibility*. Parents understand, or should understand, that, after they've created that adorable bundle of joy, they have the responsibility to turn that foot-stomping toddler into a responsible, capable adult. Because of the way most education systems have been structured, the parental responsibility has quietly shifted. Often, they're expected to be passive observers of the whole education experience. They've been quietly told that education happens somehow and

---

[2] Often attributed to Dewey, it's actually a paraphrased comment about him in James William Norman, *A Comparison of Tendencies in Secondary Education in England and the United States*. New York: Teachers College, Columbia University, 1922 — "...there has for years been a strong and growing tendency in the United States under the leadership of Dewey, and more recently of Kilpatrick, to find an educational method correlative of democracy in society with the belief that education is life itself rather than a mere preparation for life, and that practice in democratic living is the best preparation for democracy" (emphasis added).

somewhere else—in the schools, not the home, by the professionals, not the family. That's the rhetoric. In actuality, the responsibility must be shared.

Parents have traditionally been heavily involved in every aspect of education. Until the last century or two, they had absolute control—arranging apprenticeships for their sons or teaching sons the family trade; teaching home management to the daughters; and so on. Even today, until children enter kindergarten, the parents are the primary educators. When parents recognize that every moment, every experience, every opportunity from birth to adulthood, and beyond, can be part of the educational journey of their child, they take those moments seriously.

Suppose, however, the parents haven't had access to quality education. In some countries, many adults are still illiterate. In developed countries, many people feel that public education has failed them. How can we ask these parents to encourage their child to go out and explore education? How can these parents help their children develop the curiosity, the critical thinking, and the outside-myself awareness that those children need?

The Cornerstone

Back in the day, we built walls out of rocks, not steel and concrete. The cornerstone was the biggest and heaviest; it was the key to structural integrity. This book will be the cornerstone of Montessori's next great leap forward. It won't be complete or exhaustive; the plan will be refined and improved constantly along the way. You might even say this book is the first date, not the marriage.

We begin where every parent and child are and help them along to where they can be: Every parent can teach what they know and encourage children to know more. A parent can say, "We need two pineapples or ten carrots for dinner," then take the children to the market and ask them to pick up the groceries. In cooking that dinner, a parent can teach how to measure and tell time. Little things like these should not be brushed aside as insignificant events. In most circumstances, people don't take the time to see the educational value in simple home tasks that even young children can perform. To a child, those moments are gems, especially in their youngest years, not just of learning, but of bonding. We call them #MontessoriMoments.

Outside the home, parents should encourage children to see things and ask questions. If the parent doesn't know the answer, they can help the child find someone who does. As I look forward, I see Montessori providing resources to help parents understand how they can make childhood a rich learning experience. Not manuals, children need individual attention. We can, however, provide guidance on how to see what your child needs at a given moment and deal with those needs.

Childhood can become the beginning of a lifelong, self-directed learning experience. Humans are naturally curious. Parents who get into the spirit of Montessori will start asking, "How do I do this better?" We can show them how.

At some point, the child gets old enough to need some formal education. Assuming you've done everything you can at home, that might be very young. Parents then have to dialogue with educators, some of whom believe their word is law in the classroom. They won't willingly engage with "amateurs." We task ourselves with helping parents and educators create a fruitful and effective dialogue, building a solid, cooperative relationship.

Parents must understand that the professionals are always under the authority of "the management," some administrative or regulatory body. They're pushed to teach whatever they're told is the priority. They have timelines, resource limitations, mandated tests, and a host of other pressures. In the Montessori approach, the key is observation. Education can't be child-centered unless teachers actually see **those children** in the middle of **the class**. It would be much simpler if you could just ask the child about their needs and get a straight answer every time. That just doesn't happen. Teachers must observe cautiously and carefully, learning to understand how to serve each child within the parameters the "system" has set.

Teachers often feel pushed to "get through" massive amounts of information to prepare their students for tests. Sometimes, children need to be left alone for five minutes to absorb the lesson. Other times, they need to "get the wiggles out," to move, be physically active, and work off their excess energy. Sometimes, they need an idea explained in a certain way that they alone can comprehend because their brains don't work exactly like everyone else's.

Parents can help teachers understand their children so that teachers can better serve each child's needs. Teachers can explain the requirements imposed by the management or administration so parents can help their children prepare to meet those impositions.

Synergy is the idea that the whole is greater than the sum of the parts. Montessori seeks to facilitate synergy among parents, children, educators, administrators, and everyone else who has an interest in quality education.

Introduction

The Last Word

"We have the idea that education can help the development of the child, and that we adult people will give this help. That is the ordinary idea of education. This idea is not a right idea, because it concludes that the adult can help this little child very much with his own wisdom and care. The idea of education is to give to the child and to young people all the best that we have."

—Maria Montessori[3]

---

[3] Maria Montessori, *Citizen of the World: Key Montessori Readings*. Laren, The Netherlands: Montessori-Pierson Publishing Company, 2019.

Part 1
Make Montessori Available Everywhere

Chapter 1
The Problem

First Word

The secret of success is found to lie in the right use of imagination in awakening interest, and the stimulation of seeds of interest already sown by attractive literary and pictorial material, but all correlated to a central idea, of greatly ennobling inspiration—the Cosmic Plan in which all, consciously or unconsciously, serve the Great Purpose of Life.
—Maria Montessori[4]

Why Isn't Montessori Available Worldwide?

The Foundation and Floors

Maria Montessori was born in Italy in 1870. Her parents wanted her to become a teacher, but she had other ideas. Her interest lay in mathematics, and she explored engineering. She later developed an interest in biology, which led her to medical school. In 1896, she became the first female doctor in Italy. After joining the psychiatric unit of the University of Rome Medical School, she visited children committed to insane asylums. In the hospitals and clinics where she worked, Montessori observed children playing and how they experimented with games and toys to help them learn. Her observations of these

---

[4] Maria Montessori, *To Educate the Human Potential*. Madras: Kalakshetra Publications Press, 1948.

children led her to conclude that many of the issues affecting these children were not medical; they were educational.

Through extensive observation of these children, she discovered that they had an effortless ability to learn. Children could and did teach themselves, even those committed to asylums as mentally disabled. This simple, but profound, truth formed the cornerstone of her lifelong pursuit of educational reform. What has since become known as the "Montessori Method" follows one simple principle: follow the child.

In 1897, she delivered a lecture at a pedagogical meeting on the needs of children with cognitive impairments. She argued that a lack of stimulation was causing many of the patients to be hospitalized for mental and emotional conditions that could be addressed through environmental changes. Her research also led her to conclude that society, as a whole, would benefit by allowing children to develop naturally, by supporting them fully, and by understanding and meeting their individual needs. She realized that education's problem was not educational, it was social. She envisioned that a more peaceful, healthier, more compassionate society would arise from a change in how adults view children and childhood.

The Italian government supported her research: In 1898, she was named director of the State Orthophrenic[5] School by the Italian Ministry of Education, and, in 1904, she was appointed as Professor of Anthropology at the University of Rome. This work led to a request that she open a day care center in a housing project. Named *Casa*

---

[5] *Orthophrenia*, an archaic term describing 1. soundness of mind; 2. normal interpersonal relationships. From the Greek, *ortho-*, normal, and *-phrenos*, the mind. Adapted from "Orthophrenia," *TheFreeDictionary.com*. Huntingdon Valley, PA: Farlex, Inc., 2003-2025. https://medical-dictionary.thefreedictionary.com/orthophrenia, accessed 15 January 2025.

dei Bambini (Italian, "Children's House"), the world's first Montessori School opened in 1907.

At *Casa dei Bambini*, Montessori continued using the scientific method to understand how people think and learn. The school was based on her early observations and tested her methods. In the *Casa*, children learned to dress themselves by practicing buttons, ties, and laces. They taught each other to read and write with cut-out letters they could move around, and learned to count and do math with special glass beads they could hold in their hands.

Montessori's core principle, "we must meet the needs of the child," didn't come out of the conventional wisdom of the day. The Montessori Method derives from science, specifically, discerning children's needs via observation. Her observations began with the children she was working with, complemented by what she learned from the research of others.

Observation allowed her to see the natural qualities and needs of children clearly. In her first children's houses, she provided them with a variety of things to play with, allowing the children to choose their activities. She observed that children would use gadgets without any prompting, and they showed a marked preference towards gadgets over more traditional toys. As the children used these devices, she also noted their deep concentration. They also developed a sense of dignity and a love of repetition and self-discipline with no need for reward or punishment. The children came to love order without having that order imposed on them.

Montessori also noticed the children's interest in the activities they saw around them at home, like sewing clothes or washing floors. Doing these tasks helped students become more independent and became a hallmark of the Montessori philosophy that remains evident to this day. Montessori's original classrooms, with their pint-sized furniture and curious games, attracted worldwide attention. But it wasn't just the furniture that drew so much curiosity. Children in her classrooms demonstrated a new calm, peaceful manner, and cooperative attitude, which was uncommon in children's settings. It received particular notice for the initiative children took and the purpose-oriented nature of the children's activities.

Montessori observed that children learned best when they had the freedom to move, choose their own work, follow their interests, and when given time, that process repeated. In the Montessori environment, the classroom is "the prepared environment" where children are free to move around, to work where they're comfortable and feel they'll work best, and to discover through purposeful hands-on experience. Montessori learning is largely active learning, individually paced and tailored to meet the needs and interests of each child.

Based on these findings, Montessori developed a method of teaching focused on nurturing each child's potential by providing holistic (that is, well-rounded, inclusive of a full mind-body-emotion, etc.) learning experiences. All aspects of children's development and learning are intertwined in the Montessori approach and viewed as equally important. Each child's learning progress is personal, based on the unique stage of development, interest, and needs. Educators work with children one-on-one to track their progress and give support as appropriate.

Children can work with many activities independently, as most suggested Montessori apparatus is self-correcting. In Montessori's prepared environment, everything had been carefully designed so as to have a specific purpose and a place. The distinct order in the external environment assists children in developing both external and internal order and supports logical thinking throughout the process. This process can be understood as "auto-education," based on the belief that children are capable and willing to teach themselves; all they need is an eye-catching or thought-provoking stimulus to get them started. Montessori materials were developed to meet this need of liberating a child's inherent curiosity. Montessori educators create the prepared environment, then guide and encourage auto-education, trusting in the child's intrinsic motivation.

Within six years of *Casa dei Bambini*'s opening, teacher training sites and Montessori schools existed on five continents. Her first book, *The Montessori Method*, had been translated into ten languages. During her life, she oversaw the training of Montessori teachers and guided them in founding thousands of schools where the Method was core.

Maria Montessori lectured internationally for the next four decades, until she died in 1952. In the decades since her passing, the Montessori Method has continued to expand and evolve, always based on one core principle that reflects both Montessori's life as a scientist and her deep respect for the nature and promise of childhood:

Follow the child.[6]

The Walls and Roof

Pedagogy, noun, 1. the function or work of a teacher; teaching. 2. the art or science of teaching; education; instructional methods. From Greek *paidagōgía*, "the office of a child's tutor."

The Montessori Method is one of the most successful pedagogical disciplines of teaching. It carries international recognition and almost universal respect. Dr. Maria Montessori saw that children learn best through experience and that experience encourages deeper and more consistent investigation into language, mathematics, science, music, and other subjects. At the same time, it fosters social interactions

---

[6] Many thanks to Preeti Patel, Director of Programs, Montessori Global Education, and Dr. Catherine McTamaney, Associate Professor, Peabody College of Education, Vanderbilt University for the articles on which this history is based.

as children share their enthusiasm for their discoveries. Happy, self-motivated learners also form positive images of themselves as confident, successful people. To encourage this self-directed learning, Montessori has created resources specifically designed to foster this independence and love for learning from an early age.

We are "Montessori Global Education," consisting of Montessori Centre International (MCI, the trading name for St. Nicholas Montessori Training Ltd, our training college) and Montessori St. Nicholas Charity (MSN, formally known as the Montessori St. Nicholas Ltd, registered charity).

Originally established in 1954, Montessori St. Nicholas Charity has worked with governments, families, organizations, and individual educators to ensure that the Montessori approach continues to be as beneficial to modern society as it was when originally established by Montessori in the 1900s. Her vision of an education system focused on a child-led educational experience remains as necessary today as it was over a century ago.

St. Nicholas Montessori Centre was founded as an education trust to maintain the training started by Margaret Homfray and Phoebe Child, two former students of Maria Montessori. Based in Princes Gate, London, by 1971, the Centre held full-time, part-time, and Saturday courses for Montessori educators. It also established a successful Montessori setting for residential students and children. In 1978, Bridget Birts took on the leadership of St. Nicholas, serving the Montessori community until 1983. St. Nicholas Montessori Centre continued to expand and flourish, celebrating 50 years of training in 1996. In 1998, the London Montessori Centre (founded by Lesley Britton) and Montessori St. Nicholas Charity formed the Montessori Centre International (MCI), merging the work of two internationally acclaimed Montessori facilities.

Originally based in Balderton Street, London, MCI later relocated to St John's Wood, offering a blended learning method of Montessori training for educators worldwide. Since leaving a permanent London venue in 2020, MCI has focused on the delivery of training through a network of Host and Beacon training centers all over the world, strengthening our global presence and supporting a new name for the future.

Montessori St. Nicholas remains a UK-registered charitable entity to this day, ambitious and keen to promote education in every way, championing the Montessori philosophy and values as a way to benefit society, and offering support for funding and research into the value of educational practice and aligned activities around the world.

Montessori Today
The Scope

Montessori is one of many schools of thought in pedagogy and teaching methods. We have a history that's been tremendously successful for over a century. Why, then, is Montessori not universally accepted?

We describe Montessori presently, in terms of scale or reach, as "worldwide" instead of "global." Though the Method is known in most parts of the world, the Montessori movement doesn't have a presence everywhere. Not even close.

There's an almost universal understanding of existing problems in education and a near-universal appeal for better ways. Because of the challenges that arise in many countries, however, that understanding doesn't always translate to a Montessori presence. Cultural challenges often mean that parents don't take advantage of what we offer. For a variety of reasons, they won't pick it up.

This speaks directly to our vision and mission. We must overcome ignorance—in so many places, we're known by reputation, but the people don't know much more. A reputation sometimes includes numerous misconceptions. We must also overcome cultural bias—the thinking that these ideas cannot be beneficial because they come from a foreign source or a cultural model different from ours. We are committed to publicizing the truth about what Montessori can offer and including the opportunities that we can make available for the world's children.

Practicality/Realism

To be effective, the "disciples" of the Montessori Method must be trained in the Method. It's clear, specific, and intuitive, but to get the most out of it, as a teacher or as a student, you need mentoring. The metaphorical baton must be passed to you. Like the flexibility we seek for childhood education, what that support or mentoring covers will vary. It should be as personalized as possible to suit an individual educator's context, the experience with which they meet the training, and the contexts they operate within. It doesn't have to mean being part of a study group for a recognized qualification if that is not suited to their intentions and context. Our primary hope is that Montessori educators enjoy the practice and are inspired by the teachings.

There's a phrase floating about—"authentic Montessori"—which our organization chooses not to use. I honestly don't know what that phrase means. When we see images of "authentic Montessori," we see a perfect shelf, with perfect materials, all laid out in their proper place, but we don't often see children or, more significantly, we don't see activities taking place. Such displays don't show life in its vivid technicolor.

As an organization wishing to celebrate high-quality educational opportunities for children, we can admire a tidy shelf and classroom, but that, to us, isn't showing us anything that is "authentically Montessori" because that's not showing us real-life.

Life is messy; children are often unpredictable, experiences are made, and life continues as a series of episodes or interactions take place repeatedly, often with unexpected or irreplaceable results or outcomes "in the moment." We believe this should be communicated and shared—honestly portrayed, as children use things actively, and those things may land all over the place. It is part of the process, which is included in the time of activity and experience, children tidy up, what can sometimes seem like a tornado-aftermath scene, and put their things back where they belong. There are those who would have us believe that childhood must be that picture-perfect image. Childhood often isn't and sometimes can't be, so why force into existence that false image and situation? We don't want to push children into any kind of mold.

That false image becomes something of a self-limiting standard. Since many Montessorians have to be trained in a certain way, the expectation grew that their output had to look a certain way. Therefore, if you weren't trained in "proper" methods or your output didn't look "proper," then you weren't really part of that Montessori circle. Over time, these misconceptions stifle growth.

Everyone has heard the statement, "Perception is reality."

It's not. Reality is reality. What we perceive as reality affects how we deal with reality, while reality goes along its merry way without caring about our opinions. Montessorians must do a more effective job of promoting a more correct public understanding of Montessori expectations if they are to overcome these stereotypes and show the world what Montessori can truly do for students.

Prejudice

There's an inherent resistance in the educational community to labels. Putting a stake in the ground and saying, "I am X" or "I am Y" in terms of one's style of teaching may also feel "limiting." Conventional wisdom in education says we need to steer away from that hard and fast pedagogical identification because our wider sector colleagues, managers, and school career advisors tell us that the generalist approach is where we should be. In the wider sector of educational professionals, I would suggest this is similar for graduates from Reggio, Froebel, and Steiner as well. There is some justification for that attitude because it appears to give us something of a level playing field. It presents a happy medium. People shift and change, children come and go, and to be dedicated to one philosophy means the potential that society might believe this one or that one is too narrow in its focus. I think this is the primary reason the "Montessori" label has never been seen as the answer. In fact, some people ask us directly, "Isn't the Montessori brand too narrow for the changing, modern world?"

Among those who negatively view any curriculum that is labeled, well, yes, it is. However, they don't understand that Montessori is not a curriculum; it's a set of principles and practices. It's a guide or framework. It's not meant to define all the things we should be teaching. It's designed to assist teachers in opening the door and unlocking child-centered learning.

We believe, as an organization, that we must open that door and help people understand the value Montessori can add to their children and communities, child-centered principles that will be of value in any education situation.

Elitism

Sadly, prejudice often leads to misperceptions. Over our past, we have not been able to avoid this elitist label because, at some point, someone has had to put a price tag on the niche provision, representing our type of education as niche, rather than free, like state or public schools are perceived to be. "Expensive" (and what privately-owned school isn't viewed that way?) and "elitist" tend to be viewed as synonymous, especially in niche markets.

All private schools must sell themselves to prospective students' parents. In most developed countries, more often than not, parents are sold a picture of their child's future. "Get into our preschool and you'll get into the best private school. Get into our private school and you'll get into the best university. Get into our university and you'll get into the best jobs." That, too, is a misperception. But the sales pitch works, and these niche schools can now afford the pretty furniture and the pretty shelves in the classrooms, and they can afford to send every team member to the exact same training programs. Thus, many private sector providers become unattainable to the average family, and the perception of unaffordability touches every private school and setting.

Without naming any names (which I could do but wouldn't do), I've spoken to representatives of several nursery and pre-school providers with multiple locations. Many are very pleased with that "elite" tag because they fundamentally believe they can charge more for it. Some are even proud of it, and why not from a business finance model? It's an effective selling point that directly impacts their profitability and raises their standing in their communities. For them, it's a winning strategy.

But, and this should surprise no one, they become deliberately selective about which children are given access to that education because there's every reason not to open the door to "just anybody." Highly motivated, high-achieving students and families build a reputation because the schools can say, "See, we made that child into the adult he or she is today." More likely, it's the students—each one a carefully-selected experimental data point that proves a preconceived conclusion—that are making the school.

I've challenged people in these schools to consider their retail-business-like approach: "If you buy one of our widgets, we give one to an underprivileged child in Africa." Do they do anything akin to that? No, not at all of interest to them because they know where their money's coming from, a very specific market segment, and they're quite happy to serve that market segment alone.

Such attitudes give all specialized schools and programs a bad name.

Independence

Somewhere along the way (undoubtedly based on our idea that the child should take a leading role in their education), it was decided by "the system" that Montessori-trained children are less willing to work in groups. "Yes, they are good at functioning independently, but they're not team players," is a common accusation.

I have no idea where this idea came from, nor why it persists. My experience is very much the opposite. Sadly, if parents have listened to that conventional wisdom (a term, you've noticed, I don't use as a compliment), they're going to steer away from the Montessori name.

There's really very little to be said on this point beyond that. If parents fail to do what the lawyers call "their due diligence," that is, their own research, they will, almost without exception, come to erroneous conclusions because the conventional wisdom simply doesn't understand the subject.

Authenticity

I've mentioned the problem of "authentic Montessori" programs. Montessori never trademarked her methods; she wanted them available to the widest possible audience. That's led us to many different versions of Montessori. I've collected countless examples where a program might be labeled Montessori, but my experience says that it has nothing to do with Montessori's legacy. There's no global, unifying Montessori organization: no published standards and no way to rein in those who have misunderstood and misapplied Montessori theories.

There is also the challenge of Montessori's setting.

An old sage once said, "History without context is like opera without music; it's just a bunch of people running around the stage shouting in a language you don't understand." Maria Montessori was born in 1870, just a decade after the numerous Italian states became a single nation, nearly two decades before the first automobile was patented, and a century before the technological revolution that completely controls current generations. Her lifetime (the last quarter of the 19th Century and the first half of the 20th Century) saw World War I, the Spanish Flu Pandemic, the Great Depression, the rise of Fascism, World War II, and so much more. She passed away less than a decade after that last conflict. Italy, like most of the other nations—through which Montessori traveled extensively—saw political and economic turmoil as almost normal, daily business. A century after she published her early works, the changes in our society, technology, and economics almost make our world seem like a different planet.

For this reason, we don't refer to our organization as "authentic Montessori." Her fundamental concepts will outlast us all, but her program, highly effective for the needs of her generation, doesn't always meet the needs of ours and, almost certainly, won't fit the next generation or two.

For example, Montessori advocated that teachers step back from the absolute monarchy that was the average 19th-century classroom. Today, they can't step back too far:

Some factions of our population advocate alternative lifestyles that are, clearly and demonstrably, bad ideas. (And, regardless of whichever alternative you've chosen, somebody thinks your choice is a bad idea!)

There are statutory requirements imposed by local and national governments that must be met.

We've seen a rise in students with what the UK system calls "Special Educational Needs and Disabilities" in state or public schools, with professional referral and intervention initiatives to consider. (This is one of the things that Maria Montessori hoped for in working with special-needs children in Italy, to get as many as possible into the mainstream of life.)

She advocated for designated three-hour blocks of uninterrupted time to be "allocated" for child-directed activity. During this time, children had the freedom to explore, attempt, master, interact, experience and try out areas of the "curriculum" that took their interest. The teacher observes and learns more about their individual needs. Few modern school schedules allow for that kind of activity period.

Some have decided that the definition of "authentic Montessori" is so narrow that they end up tossing out a multitude of benefits on the ill-informed notion that "it doesn't fit the here and now." Instead, we seek "sustainable Montessori." We've tried to take Montessori's principles and adapt them to modern needs and situations in such a way that they'll still be applicable decades into the future.

Our Target Market

One might've expected me to start a book like this by defining our target market: Who am I writing to?

The Problem

An excellent question, but I put off answering it until I'd laid the groundwork so the reader would understand my context. One of the first questions my publisher asked was, "Are you writing principally to parents or educators?"

I replied, "Can't it be both?"

In preparing this book, I spoke to a colleague who drew an interesting analogy: Everyone's heard about quarks, even people with little knowledge of sub-atomic physics. We know there are up and down, top and bottom, strange and charmed quarks, but, to most of us, those are just funny names in a branch of science not known for its humor. What are they, really, and what do they do?

I think he hit the nail on the head. Are we **teaching** Montessori? Are we **being** Montessori? Are we **practicing** Montessori? For the average parent or teacher, the answer is, "Oh, yes, I've heard of Montessori, they have those schools."

To alleviate this confusion, we, as an organization, choose to come at this confusion with bold confidence.

"Come and learn about Montessori!" is our open invitation to, well, everybody.

The door isn't closed; we are not elitist or exclusionary. Some so-called Montessori organizations thrive on that exclusivity. We respond by reminding them of her own statement:

> My educational method has grown from... revelations, given by the children. All the details included in the Method, have come from the efforts to follow the child. The new path has been shown us. No one knows exactly how it arose, it just

came into being and showed us the new way. It has nothing to do with any educational method of the past, nor with any educational method of the future. It stands alone as the contribution of the child himself. It cannot have come from an adult person; the thought, the very principle that the adult should stand aside to make room for the child, could never have come from the adult. Anyone who wants to follow my method must understand that he should not honor me but follow the child as his leader.

—Maria Montessori[7]

By experiencing the Montessori Method and then seeing students succeed with it, we hope to break the cycle of the education industry's conventional wisdom, that families and wider community (or "actual educators") have no place in educating children. Educators come from our communities; they pass through some sort of certification to become educators. Many are also parents. We want to give them the confidence to say, "I am an educator, a professional, and I can choose the framework that guides me in my profession."

Parents, meanwhile, are paying for their children's education through taxes or tuition. If they don't see value in what we offer, they won't support it. Moreover, they won't approach members of Parliament or other legislators to push them to change how education works. Likewise, parents can be "professional" even if they aren't in the profession. They can adopt the philosophy and take advantage of that support framework. They can develop confidence in their ability to provide quality education to their children.

---

[7] Maria Montessori, "The First Casa dei Bambini," *Montessori150.org*. Amsterdam: Association Montessori Internationale (also known as "The Rome Speech 1942"). https://montessori150.org/maria-montessori/first-casa-dei-bambini, accessed 28 March 2025.

The Problem

As I've looked at Montessori as a movement and as a training organization, our statistics say 85 percent of our graduates identify as career-changers. Montessori is often found by people who have had their children and are now seeking something better for them.

A common scenario begins when the children get a bit older and a bit more self-sufficient. Their mother often comes to us to retrain and become a Montessori educator. That has happened so often that I don't think enough is said about it. It's quite significant that the parental experience motivates so many parents to change careers.

So, this book will slant somewhat toward a parental audience but include professional teachers because they are equally vital to the program.

As an organization, we need to be wise about our messaging. This book will be the part of that message most readily available to parents. It will also be one of several ways we reach out to the professionals.

We want to recognize the interdependence of home and classroom and create synergy. Co-creation, one might call it. That's why the concept of curricula so concerns me. Often, it's written by people who aren't educators or subject experts, and, in such cases, the child's voice is missing. When we tell children what they need to learn, and we refuse all debate, they've got no engagement as to why they're learning or how they're learning or even the context of how their education applies to them. Why, in that scenario, should they care?

Conventional wisdom doesn't allow children to have the freedom they need to open their minds, explore what interests them, and nurture curiosity. We want to bring the excitement of discovery into every child's life. That has to begin long before they hit the classroom, meaning it's up to the parents to nurture that curiosity. Too many classrooms push students to memorize names, dates, places, and events so they can regurgitate them on exams. That is knowledge, but it isn't education.

As the new CEO of Montessori Global Education, I'm looking forward to the next 10 or 20 years and to facilitating a long-lasting portfolio of services and support programs that will, we hope, fundamentally change the way parents and educators view the home and classroom experiences.

My vision is a world where the power of Montessori education is available to everyone.

The Last Word

> Once the teacher understands that mysterious powers exist within the child, and that these reveal themselves spontaneously through the child's activities, his attitude will change, no longer being that of a superior toward an inferior; for he will realize that here is a treasure that must be allowed to yield benefits. Humanity is in dire need of this new type of educators.
>
> —Maria Montessori[8]

---

[8] Maria Montessori, *Citizen of the World: Key Montessori Readings*. Laren, The Netherlands: Montessori-Pierson Publishing Company, 2019.

Chapter 2
The Solution

THE FIRST WORD

The child has infinite possibilities which were not known before. Little children have lived in the world for thousands and thousands of years and no one has ever been aware of them.
—Maria Montessori[9]

What Is Child-Centered Learning?

Before we embark on an explanation of how to solve the challenges that face us, let us dive deeper into the concept:

Child-centered learning is more than just a catchall phrase for warm, friendly classrooms. It's more than designing curricula based on understanding children's learning trajectories or their culture. As noted earlier, most people who look into a classroom see a *class*. Child-centered learning looks into a classroom and sees 10 or 20 or whatever number of **students**.

Today's educational environments increasingly consider developmentally-appropriate practices and incorporate learning and play to respond to the emotional, physical, artistic, social, intellectual, and cultural needs of children. Child-centered learning does all those things, but, at its best, it is a highly individualized, holistic approach

---

[9] Maria Montessori (edited by Annette M. Haines), *The 1946 London Lectures, Volume 17 of The Montessori Series*. Laren, The Netherlands: Montessori-Pierson Publishing Company, 2012.

where teachers are more than lecturers or testers and parents are more than bystanders.

The most developed models of child-centered learning allow each child to choose their own activities, content, and topics in ways that satisfy that child's curiosity. Children are naturally motivated to explore the world around them, seeking to understand and enjoy it. Such environments provide relevant, engaging, and open-ended activities, and allow for ample time to play and explore, encouraging children to explore more.

Children understand things when they have multiple opportunities to engage with those things, especially when supported by valid tasks, where they experience content in holistic ways: exploring with hands-on, personally relevant tasks, allowing them to go deeply into ideas that interest them. This affirms the child's vital role in their own journey of discovery.

Parents and teachers fill two roles in this journey, as observers and guides. As observers, they come to know the child. As guides, they help the child make the best use of their learning. Also, as mentioned, parents and teachers see the child in vastly different circumstances. Close communication between them increases how well they both understand the child's needs, strengths, weaknesses, and so on.

Teachers in child-centered spaces design learning opportunities based on their knowledge of children's development. Teachers don't necessarily plan out what each child will learn over any given period. Instead, they observe carefully. They assess by monitoring and documenting children's activities, their varying interests and curiosity levels, their prosocial behaviors, and their growth across time.

The Solution

Child-centered learning spaces differ from the standard classroom environments, where teachers create activities to be presented to a large group of children. Child-centered spaces begin with the unique aspects of each child and build opportunities that match individual interests with experiences that challenge and propel learning. Teachers design environments that engage and provide structure and boundaries to make sure activities are safe, focused, and joyful.

The Montessori Method is one of the original "child-centered learning" models that emerged over the last century. Montessori wrote, "Free activity makes children happy. We can see how happy they are, but it is not the fact that they are happy that is important; the important thing is that a child can construct a man through this free activity."[10] In the Montessori Method, a child's happiness isn't the end goal of the classroom; it's a way of assessing their level of engagement in learning activities.

Research over the last hundred years has strengthened Maria Montessori's theories. That research confirms that child-centered models enhance cognitive development; boost critical thinking skills, encourage collaboration, and challenge children to prove or disprove what they think they know. Research also suggests that children show stronger social competence, enhanced self-esteem, and awareness of their ability to persist through challenging tasks and to achieve understanding. In short, it helps children become independent, confident, and creative learners. Montessori also wrote, "There is not just a need for happier schools, schools where the children are free to do as they like or schools where they use certain materials: education today needs reform. If education is to prepare man for the present, and the immediate future, he will need a new orientation towards the environment."[11]

---

[10] *Ibid.*
[11] *Ibid.*

Montessori for All—Accessibility and Perception

One of the most significant challenges we face is getting the door open.

If someone's found their way to our methodology, whether they know the Montessori name or not, we're willing to work with them to identify what best practices are already being implemented. We want to flip the switch, so to speak, turning the light on to what else the Method can do. "How," we ask, "can the synergy of a Montessori approach benefit those concerned in your situation?"

We don't ask, "Were you trained? Where were you trained? How many hours of practice have you done? Which books did you read?" It's not about training somebody to become a Montessorian, which used to be the definition of being part of the Montessori Method.

Our definition is about recognizing the practice in action, wherever it's making a difference today and, potentially, in the future. We find that identifying practices that people are already using, even if those folks don't identify them as Montessori, opens the door because they already see something of what the Method can do.

There are still umpteen countries in the world where little or nothing of the Method is prevalent. In those places, no educators get training, and no children benefit from it. I doubt anyone will accidentally read a book and think, "Oh, that's a great idea." In our experience, most of those who find Montessori discover it when they're looking for an individualized program. They've identified a need, and they're not seeing, among the teaching programs already available to them, a system that works for them. We sometimes get messages like, "I'm in such-and-such a location and my child is unhappy every day," or "My child feels, you know, controlled, and that's not the way that we live our lives." When someone finds Montessori, there's usually a specific motivation behind their search.

Where Montessori is not prevalent in a country, there are gloriously happy people because they have a lovely new baby, and now, they're thinking about doing the best for that child. How do we provide access for them? How do we engage those parents? Like any commercial business entering a new market, we need to earn our market share.

Earning new market share is a tall order for any business, one that we're looking to meet head-on. It influences everything that we do, especially the language that we use to promote and market. We've got to be welcoming, we've got to convince people we exist to help everybody, and that we can. Couple the ignorance with misperceptions or pre-judgements, which are the backbone of human skepticism, and the challenge may seem insurmountable. It isn't. It'll take time and patience, and many we talked to won't buy in immediately. We expect that. My research suggests that, in some countries, elite nurseries already claim the name Montessori. That makes it more challenging because you're not just introducing the brand to new families, you're introducing it to families who'll say, "Oh, you're from the school down the road that I can't afford."

No, we're not.

Adapting to Survive

Montessori doesn't have, and should never have, a unified, standardized program.

That may surprise some readers, and some Montessori practitioners, but it's one reason why this book is so important to me. I hope to take the Montessori Method beyond the traditional Montessori School and into government-run schools, private schools, charter schools, home schools, prisons, hospitals, businesses, wherever anybody wants to apply these principles.

Recall the vision: *A world where the power of Montessori education is available to everyone.*

Not every child—everyone! There's a difference. Montessori is learning for life, and learning should not end with a graduation or two.

We recognize that some schools will be quite happy to absorb our Method, even though they never describe themselves as a Montessori facility. I'm fine with that. We know there will be schools that call themselves Montessori but decline our approach. I'm fine with that, too.

We have set ourselves to move toward a place where Montessori means continuous professional teacher development, always seeking new and better ways to serve the children's needs. (Likewise, continuous corporate trainer development means always seeking new and better ways to serve the employees' needs.) We want to see every educator regularly refreshing themselves in educational theory and practice through discussion with other educators.

We recognize that Montessori is one among numerous schools of thought. We respect what they're trying to accomplish and wish them well. That said, I will state absolutely that, among all educational philosophies calling themselves child-centered, my research says Montessori is the best approach. Its flexibility is one of the key value points of the Method.

If we wanted to unify the Montessori movement, we'd need to get all the various practitioner groups together, establish a global authority, adopt a set of rules or standards (in effect, adopt a canon of scripture), agree to specific practices (the interpretation of that scripture, if you will), and, finally, adopt penalties for failure to comply (some form of excommunication). If Montessori wanted that, she would've trademarked her program. Her whole point would've been immediately lost if we went this route.

One might say, "All Montessoris need to look the same to be good, then, don't they?" We're saying, "No, that's not the case." Montessori is about putting principles into practice in such a variety of circumstances that we can't all look the same. We need to adapt the Method to local needs.

We're confident that Montessori Global Education has done the best research that can be done and has synthesized our practices into a plan that Montessori would support. Our pillars and practices are our best guess as to how to serve today's children, founded on her work from a century ago. Also, we feel she'd approve of our expanding her work to include nontraditional locations such as in homes and community scenarios.

We've tested and continue to test this practice in non-educational settings and with "non-educators"—parents and corporate professionals. We've spent 70 years training Montessorians who were looking for a realistic Montessori practice. We've done that successfully; we know that the program works.

Our graduates, however, are a fixed number of people, and it's not enough to meet our vision. Every educational department or ministry, in every country that we've spoken with, now sees a recruitment and retention crisis. If that's the case, and it clearly is, somebody, somewhere, at some point, has got to realize the impossibility of training through the same model. If we're to meet a worldwide need, we need to do it differently.

Among other things, we need to instill in people the concept that learning is a lifelong journey and build the process of learning into a habit. We need to constantly develop, evolve, and assess ourselves against Montessori's writings. Self-reflection is a key to growth within the Montessori Method.

Refocus the Lens—Our Pillars in Practice
Pedagogical Principles

Vertical Grouping: The grouping of children of various ages, stages, and years of schooling; when together, learning has "texture." Different interests, skills, and personalities blend together much like a "real" society or community. It has been suggested that, in such a space, individuals will be more likely to compete against themselves, rather than each other, and they learn to be unafraid of making mistakes. This promotes the development of a growth mindset, an essential outlook for ongoing development.

The Work Cycle: Ideally, a block of uninterrupted focus time where learners can independently follow their interests.

The Favorable Environment: Physical design to accommodate and facilitate positive learning experiences. Smaller furniture, designed for and manageable by children, organized with shelves but taking access considerations into account.

An Empathetic Educator: The ideal facilitator in a learning experience.

Key Fundamentals or Principles

Supporting the Child as an Active Learner
Respecting the Inner Life of the Child
Trusting the Child's Inner Motivation
Providing Freedom Within Limits
Encouraging the Child's Inner Discipline

The Solution

The idea of following the child focuses on a message: It doesn't need tools and tricks or gadgets. It doesn't even need a roof or walls or any type of defined space. It needs a person and a child (preferably a group of children), and attention to the moment when teaching can take place. It also needs to recognize when something's not connecting, such as when the child is doing X even though I'm expecting them to be doing Y.

An oversimplified example: I expected a child to be cleaning up his toys, but he's got his mind on learning to tie his shoes. I see him tie his right shoe; should I tell him to tie his left shoe as well? Not necessarily. They are slightly different activities, and his little brain might really need a chance to repeat tying that right shoe repeatedly, because that's what children need neurologically to make that new pathway that they can repeat with confidence.

If I demand that he move to the left shoe, he thinks he's failed. He needs repetition to solidify the process in his growing mind. So, you might ask, if he's successfully tied his right shoe once, should I make him do that shoe ten or twelve times? Also, no. He needs to decide for himself when he's got that activity down pat. Then, he'll want to try tying his left shoe.

We, as educators, need to find moments when the child wants to deal with challenges. In the morning, we rush to get to work or get children to school or a hundred other things. Mornings are generally not good times for parents. We need to take advantage of times with few distractions. After dinner could be such a time. The child also then learns when it's a suitable time to ask for help. When that quiet time comes, we can encourage learning, perhaps noting, "I saw that you tried really hard with that shoe today..." As a follow-up, if he picks the shoes, it's because that's in his mind at that moment, and that's the right place for him. He wants to learn. Maybe he wants to try again or refine his skills. He may ask for help if he hasn't figured it out on his own, unfolding in that moment may well be "work," daily activity, and evolution of life-skill, becoming "play." He may, of course, immediately put a small stone into the shoe and then continue to seek out as many other small items as possible to squash further into the shoe, or something similar that it totally unexpected, as he takes ownership over that learning process, and uncovers more ways to engage with the "material" or "play" with his new "toy."

As children grow, the concept of independence forms naturally in their minds. They see rain, for example, and want to experience it. They won't want to need an adult or ask for help getting their shoes on; they want to get out and feel the rain on their faces and maybe jump into a mud puddle or two. Once they've learned to put on their own shoes, they can go to their friends and family and show that they're ready to play in the rain.

Many people miss this because, in the Montessori Method, they see children with brooms and brushes and they think "work." If the children do it willingly, it's "play." This concept is also great for parents because it's a lot of work to constantly think and plan, "What am I doing with them next?" If one observes over time, one learns to see what the children want and how to turn these moments into learning experiences.

Professionalism → Empowering → Self-Direction

Among mathematical symbols, the right-pointed arrow means "yields," it means if the things to the left of the arrow happen (usually a formula of some type), it becomes, creates or produces what's on the right.

For example, $4H+O_2 \rightarrow 2H_2O$ is short for "combine four hydrogen molecules (one hydrogen atom each) with one oxygen molecule (two oxygen atoms), yielding two water molecules (two hydrogen atoms and one oxygen atom each)."

The Solution

In the UK and, from what I've seen and heard, the situation is similar in other countries. Young men and women go into teaching with a bright spark, lots of enthusiasm, lots of grand plans, but they don't run their program. Someone else runs their school and pays the bills. Regulators get involved or statutory bodies get involved, and, slowly but surely, the educator is up to their eyes in, "I've got to teach this now. They're assessing it on Friday. I've got to hurry through this."

Then, along comes an administrator, "Oh, sorry, the school bell's rung and you've run out of time."

The limitations put on schools by forces outside the classroom take over so quickly that we see the love that inspires people to take on the challenge doesn't get the time and space it needs to grow and flourish, and it's replaced by automated lessons and rote memorization. We strongly believe that teachers must be free to practice professionally. **Professionalism** means several things:

1. To be treated as the technical experts they are—trained, certified, trusted.
2. To be respected when they stand up for their students and say, "I know you want me to teach this, but they need me to teach that and that."
3. Paid what their contribution to society is worth.

Certainly, at the university level, teaching can be very profitable. At the early years, primary and secondary levels, however, most do it for the love of the work, not for the money, so point three is a bit of a long shot. The others are not.

If the enthusiasm for the work is to continue long term, the teachers need to feel they are trusted professionals. If they don't, they can be underpaid for doing vast numbers of other things. This is why the education sector sees a recruitment and retention crisis. Teachers need to feel they have the power to do their jobs, but the controlling entities—school boards, legislators, advocates—keep getting in the way.

Teacher empowerment says, "We give you the right to control your classroom." It is the controlling entities saying, "Here are the goals we work toward, make it happen any way you need to."

Empowerment has become a buzzword in leadership training circles, describing how the authority to make decisions drops from the top tier of organizations to individuals and small teams. Teacher empowerment can be a great first step toward greater success.

But empowerment only goes so far. We've been talking about letting children lead their own education. That's not empowerment. That's not granting children the right to be curious about this or that. The children are instinctively curious about their world. We can't give them what they already have, unless we're trying to control them by falsely suggesting they need our permission.

We begin by telling teachers, "Observation is key; the answer is right in front of you."

We then tell children, "We know you're curious; show us what you want to learn about today."

This provides opportunities for self-direction by the child and sensitive discernment by the teacher.

When both teacher and student internalize these concepts, the resulting classroom experience is one where **#OpportunityEmpowers**.

Our Future
Ongoing Support

- We Want to Be Your Go-To for the Next Steps.
- Continual Professional Development Should be Attractive.
- Learning for Life.
- The Subtle Art of Observation.
- A Way In / Language of the Masses, The Industry, The Sector.

Listen and Recognize

1. Dialogue and Feedback with Community Members.
2. Provide a Platform for Sharing among Community Members.
3. Amplify Single Voices to the Powers that Be.

The Last Word

We depart from our custom of quoting Maria Montessori in favor of a concise expression of a key point of this chapter. Before gaining fame as the creator of *Star Trek*, Gene Roddenberry was a police officer in Los Angeles, California. Some of his earliest writing jobs were helping his superiors write speeches and contributing to *The Beat*, the LAPD's magazine, in which he wrote:

There are seven basic obligations that, when practiced, put an occupation into the realm of a profession:

1. A duty to serve mankind generally rather than self, individuals or groups.
2. A duty to prepare as fully as practicable for services before entering active practice.
3. A duty to continually work to improve skills by all means available and to freely communicate professional information gained.

4. A duty to employ full skill at all times regardless of considerations of personal gain, comfort or safety, and at all times to assist fellow professionals upon demand.
5. A duty to regulate practice by the franchising of practitioners, setting the highest practicable intellectual and technical minimums; to accept and upgrade fellow professionals solely upon considerations of merit; and to be constantly alert to protect society from fraudulent, substandard or unethical practice through ready and swift disenfranchisement.
6. A duty to zealously guard the honor of the profession by living exemplary lives publicly and privately, recognizing that injury to a group serving society injures society.
7. A duty to give constant attention to the improvement of self-discipline, recognizing that the individual must be the master of himself to be the servant of others.

—Eugene Wesley "Gene" Roddenberry[12]

---

[12] *The Beat*, September 1952, quoted in David Alexander, *Star Trek Creator: The Authorized Biography of Gene Roddenberry*. New York City: Roc Books (now an imprint of Penguin Group), 1994.

Part 2
Demonstrate, Convincingly, the Impact Montessori Can Have on Every Child

Chapter 3
The Problem

First Word

> *Although this method bears my name, it is not the result of the efforts of a great thinker who has developed his own ideas. My method is founded on the child himself. Our study has its origins in the child. The method has been achieved by following the child and his psychology.*
> —Maria Montessori[13]

Why Isn't Montessori's Impact Understood?

As we reflect back on the misperceptions that we discussed earlier, we see a lengthy list that forms a barrier to really understanding the whole Montessori idea. In that discussion, I wrote:

> Everyone has heard the statement, "Perception is reality."

> It's not. Reality is reality. What we perceive as reality affects how we deal with reality, while reality goes along its merry way without caring about our opinions.

Erroneous perceptions still exist among many who think they know what Montessori is all about—who it's for, where it's used, who can access it, and so on. All they "know" is that Montessori is not for them. Once the audience draws that conclusion, they will never be able to

---
[13] *The 1946 London Lectures, op. cit.*

read Maria Montessori's work. They won't even take notice of her inspirational quotes because they already "know" Montessori can't serve their situation. They've made assumptions—they've created perceptions (misperceptions, really)—and are not likely to challenge those misperceptions on their own.

We know that many people around the globe are looking for something better for their children—individualization, that recognition that their child is a person who's emerging into their own state of 'humanhood,' for lack of a better term. We know there's a desire for the impact that Montessori education can have on children. However, the Montessori Method is considered an "alternative education" program. General confidence in so-called "alternative education" is lacking because parents are perpetually nervous:

- "If I go down this route with my child, am I closing off other routes in the future?"
- This isn't the school that most other children in our neighborhood go to.
- What does Montessori mean?
- I went through the public school system, and I turned out alright.

What's been peddled in popular conversation about education so permeates that conversation that there's little room left for talk of alternatives, and what talk there is can include a lot of incorrect information. The Montessori movement has contributed to this by putting its stamp on alternative education choices. Previous incarnations of our organization have said that we want to be **the** alternative to the public education system that presently exists. But alternative education has all sorts of strange and wonderful stories and tales about it, both what and how it provides that learning.

To start a conversation, it becomes sticky because you have a number of educators who are trying their best to be child-focused, child-led, and child-centered, but even they start to question how that can work when you've got statutory requirements and regulators and all the rest of the challenges we've discussed. I think that, if we can succeed in broadening people's perception, allowing them to come and see that Montessori is for all, they can say, from their own experience, that our approach is genuinely able to provide quality support and training.

We need to develop means of raising our profile in a way that gives them confidence, which will lead to a full-circle moment, where people renew the reputation they once saw in Maria Montessori's work a century ago. That will most likely start when parents see the benefits for themselves. Parents are asking for child-centered education. Our vision is a world where every family has access to that level of education.

Getting in the Door

We can't effectively focus on the teachers alone; they aren't the final decision-makers. We can't effectively focus on the school boards alone; they are politicians, and politicians have agendas. We must therefore focus on marketing directly to parents. They are the consumers, the people who pay for education more broadly, and many of them are the people serving on local school boards and working in the classrooms.

So, while we host professional-level conversations with teachers and board members to reset, as it were, their understanding of Montessori, we bring parents into the conversation, giving it a new edge. Only part of the parent population has negative preconceptions about Montessori. The majority have heard the name and little more. Overcoming a lack of knowledge is a lesser uphill battle than overcoming prejudice. We present Montessori to them as an opportunity for their children to learn on an individual basis; a chance for them to see learning in action. This creates an opportunity for their children to have educational freedom within whatever limits we must operate, while feeling secure and confident as they build their independence.

Montessori has one spectacular advantage: This educational freedom doesn't need to be negotiated or sold to parents. No parent will say, "I don't want my child to be happy at school," especially when so few of those parents were. So, if we can present our Method in ways that show children enjoying education as we help them develop those basic functional skills, parents will buy into the idea with confidence.

Additionally, we present this as something that they can do at home in simple ways. The independence we offer isn't held for ransom in the classroom. It's the examples of organic, recurring, family-led learning and teaching that we presented in previous chapters, taught by parents every minute of every day from the moment of birth through, I repeat, the normal things every family does.

We don't want to be seen as going cap-in-hand from professional organization to professional organization, when we know many of those associations have closed their doors to us. Neither do we want to "go behind their backs" by marketing exclusively to parents for the purpose of getting them to attack and overturn existing scholastic curricula and leadership. We want parents to understand what Montessori is all about and see them go to school boards and say, "This is what our children deserve." Or perhaps, to run for a seat on those boards and bring their commitment to the Method with them.

Ultimately, we need to overcome the common lack of knowledge and the more common lack of understanding about Maria Montessori's work and goals. By reaching out to parents effectively and by developing strong ties to parents, we can circumvent most misperceptions. We also firmly believe that we will appeal to a lot of educators who've struggled to find honesty or truth within their pedagogy. If they look, they will see that Montessori does add value (and perhaps even validity) to whatever their teaching practice is striving to achieve.

Proof of Concept

Every adult needs a specific, universal set of skills to function most effectively in a civilized society. These include curiosity, resilience, determination, and a sense of personal independence. Those are more difficult to measure than tangible things like test scores. We know that assessment outcomes would have to be measured in diverse ways to determine success. We, along with parents, might be championing success markers like, "My child's having a marvelous time at school" or "I feel that they've had a worthwhile day when they don't come home screaming or sullen" or it might be as straight-forward as "my children can now tie their own shoes!"

This is solid developmental teaching—parents who see real-world benefits instead of high scores on standardized tests that measure skills they may never use. Regulators (administrators, board politicians, testing companies, politicians, and others) don't want to hear that so-and-so tied their shoes for the first time, or that so-and-so had made three friends when they usually spend their days screaming that they don't want to come into school.

Current educational leadership, as a whole, doesn't want to hear anything but benchmarks they can use to demonstrate to the rest of the world that their school succeeds by graduating "superior" students. We, therefore, have a disconnect in many countries, if not all of them. Standardized assessments have little to do with the real-life learning that students obtain through educational experiences that reflect real-life experience.

The educational experience is the life those children are now living. There's a rhetoric that's been pushed for a long time: "We're preparing children for life after graduation." It seems that most of the current education has as an underlying theme, "We're preparing them for the future they dream of." A legitimate goal, but we ask, why aren't we preparing them for the life they're living now? When I speak directly to children's voices—youth advocates—they're desperate for people to understand that school is the life children are leading right now. So, we don't just engage our voice for future years; we're living in the now with the children. "We're trying to prepare them for adulthood" is something I hear constantly from educators and parents. This is a good goal, but let me suggest an alternative:

- In preparation for life, children learn to look critically at their work and become adept at recognizing, correcting, and learning from their errors.

- After intensive initial support, when children first enter a Montessori environment, educators slowly support children in becoming more independent learners by providing them with an environment and resources that support them.

That is the key—doing it now, not later. If they can't do it as children, it's not likely they'll be able to do it as adults.

Philosophy & Pedagogy: Security, Time & Effort

If students start building their knowledge in a space where they feel safe, they won't be scared of learning. If they're not scared of learning or forced along a certain path but are able to find their own style of learning, they'll emerge with a sense of ownership over their knowledge acquisition process. (Not that a term like "knowledge acquisition process" would mean anything to them.)

The Problem

If you ask a group of adults spanning a wide age range, they'll say they have some memory of being told to sit down and learn or something like that. They'll remember school's negatives, especially its restrictive nature. I imagine a future where, if you asked them what they remember about learning, they'll remember rich experiences of exploring, investigating, and researching in a laboratory, through reading a book or seeing a video, and, if possible, going somewhere to immerse themselves in the real world.

I remember many days when we sat in rows, textbooks open, watching three or four of my fellow students fall asleep because that wasn't their learning style. Those memories have become my experience, rather than anything to do with the content that class was supposed to share.

I see a shift happening. This is the hope that we at Montessori have for generations of future children:

- That they'll already have had a changed learning experience at home;
- That it won't be a challenge for them to stay attuned to learning;
- That parents will be on this journey with their children, changing their generational feelings about education in general;
- That parents will experience all this with their children, learning along with them.

We foresee generations of children remembering their parents helping them in learning and gathering educational experience, rather than earlier generations, who experience parental figures demanding completion of homework or rote learning of facts that they were just meant to "get on with," in isolation, in silence, and likely with no additional support.

As one of my colleagues recently said in an interview:

> This is perhaps one of the most misunderstood concepts of the Montessori Philosophy and Pedagogy. When the idea of freedom is raised in a Montessori environment, there are visions of chaos and a free-for-all; the reality could not be further from this.
>
> Children within the environment are offered a number of freedoms such [as] time, choice, movement, opportunity to work alone or in a group, to name a few, within agreed (with the children, not set by adults) boundaries.
>
> This allows for autonomy and independence seen in very few places leading to an engaged, calm and supportive environment in which children thrive physically, emotionally, cognitively and academically—with children being active participants and not mere bystanders in the learning and developmental journey.
> —Preeti Patel, Director of Programs, Montessori Global Education[14]

By starting the Montessori Method at home with very young children, parents can begin teaching small things that children need to know, including tying their shoes, sweeping the floor, putting toys away, and becoming independent doers. Hopefully, that will lead those children into a mindset of wanting to become independent thinkers and doers. If so, they'll want to explore sciences, arts, and more; to find out why things work, instead of just how they work; what happened, why it happened, and why it affects them. More importantly, this curiosity and desire to explore will never leave them.

---

[14] Janet King, "Exploring Montessori: Trusting in a Child's Motivation and Abilities," *NCFE.org.uk*. Newcastle upon Tyne, England, UK: NCFE, undated. https://www.ncfe.org.uk/all-articles/exploring-montessori/, accessed 6 February, 2025.

Authentic versus Sustainable

As we study Maria Montessori's works, we get clearer insight into her thinking. Even those who've read only a little bit of her work see a clear mindset there. What's her starting point? The close observation of a child is, and always will be, the first article of faith of the Montessori Method.

She didn't spend her time writing pictures of the future in any detail. She spent her time in the here-and-now, saying, in effect, "I have seen something special and noteworthy; this is a way into understanding children." She didn't do that vision-thing of predicting what might be 100 years later or trying to describe what the world would or should look like. She then focused on the situation and needs of the children in her care. That gives me confidence in saying she wasn't an absolutist. She didn't feel qualified to tell us how to accomplish her goals; she did what she could in her society and trusted us to do our best in our society, aided by her experiences. Let's view this from another perspective:

I've already mentioned the difficulty with the idea of an *authentic* Montessori way of teaching:

- Can we utilize exactly the techniques and methods she used? No, it would be impossible (not to mention ridiculous) to re-create a Montessori classroom from the 1930s. People would never sign on to it.

- She had almost none of the technology on which we depend, and which parents and students expect. Neither did she have the administrators, legislators, and others that we need to satisfy.

Therefore, we've set out to create a *sustainable* Montessori: We respect and emulate Maria Montessori's teachings, adapting them to the changing needs and wants of our generation.

Then

I spoke to a colleague who started in public school in the mid-1960s. He remembers watching numerous movies—real films on reel-to-reel film projectors (pun intended). He even learned how to run the machine and became the unofficial class projectionist. He remembers school assemblies where outside individuals would lecture and demonstrate. One particularly memorable assembly involved several Native Americans who demonstrated their culture. He was among a few students called on to participate. (As a reward, they were given "Indian" names—his was called "Giggling Porcupine" because he couldn't stop laughing.) His best memories were of field trips to some of the most exciting places in and around New York City, where he was born. These were opportunities unavailable to Montessori's generation, just as my colleague's generation was denied the internet, video-conferencing, and a host of other things.

Now

Our perception, which we call **Montessori Global Education**, understands that, as time evolves, as technology and other things become part of life, they'll become part of what we deliver.

However, returning to the perception problem, not all of it is misperception. There remain a few "traditionalist Montessorians," those who would have us believe that we need to hold fast to the original Method. I'm being very honest when I say they're living in the Dark Ages. If Maria Montessori had our level of tech when she was writing, she would've embraced it. I see that clearly in everything she wrote.

"There wasn't tech then, so there shouldn't be tech now," or any similar statement, is a self-limiting declaration. Montessori was categorically opposed to limiting her children's opportunities to learn, so how could we, in good conscience, limit our opportunities to teach? It simply makes no sense.

She was on the cutting edge of a changing attitude in education. Logic demands that she would assume someone's going to come along and learn something she didn't know and add it to her program. She observed so she could meet individual needs. We've observed for the last 100 years and now have mountains of data she couldn't access, especially about students with rare or unique needs. How could we not include the knowledge for which she is best known when working with marginalized students?

The same is true of tools. For example, the cost of creating audio-visual works was prohibitive, even a few years ago. Young entrepreneurs are literally making a living blogging while they're still in high school. It doesn't have to be Hollywood-class professionalism in anything. Students are recreating historical events, excerpting literature, hosting political debates, teaching methods of scientific inquiry, and more. It's all about involvement, and what's more involving than creation?

It's also a source of pride, a source of expression, and a chance for parents to show interest and engage with what their children are doing, to comment on it, to encourage them, and to do things with them. Parents can and should slip quietly into guide mode and become part of that creative process, which is good for the child's education. It's even better for bonding parent and child, and that is an achievement for both.

What is true of audio-visual is true of other subjects. America, Britain, and many other countries have numerous sites of living history that recreate life from centuries past. Experience living people living as they did in the past, and explaining the realities of life. Could it generate an appreciation in children of what they have?

One can only hope so!

The Downsides

Over the last 60 years, many generations of technology have come and gone. Some of them had distressingly short lifespans. Changing or upgrading tech has costs, and few schools or families can afford to keep up with the "latest and greatest." Parents and schools have to make tough decisions about those expenses and justify them to administrators, school boards, politicians, voters (not all of whom are parents). It can be a tough sell.

I think there's a timing element to those discussions. Certainly, in the UK, those who regulate education move very slowly. They're not ahead-of-the-curve types in any way, shape, or form.

As I write this, the Prime Minister has just announced a goal to become an AI leader, seemingly with little awareness that the UK hasn't led in anything significantly tech-related in decades or centuries. Personally, I can't see a workable plan for such integration and involvement. That announcement was the typical knee-jerk reaction that politicians are famous for. It may win votes, but it's rarely something that we actually see happening.

I understand that regulators serve two vital functions: Getting the job done properly while guarding the public funds entrusted to them. In that respect, I don't have a problem with them moving a little slowly, because each new iteration of expected "enhancement" processes, tools, and technology brings with it new challenges. It takes time to identify and develop countermeasures to those new considerations and the positioning of those "assets" in the learning and teaching arena. Concerns relating to the presence and impact of "fake news" and "deepfakes," for example, seem to be reaching pandemic proportions on the internet. Google those words, and it might return 10 million or 100 million or even 1 billion websites, with the vast majority illustrating just how inappropriate, harmful, and shockingly "accessible" these sites are, which we don't want children to visit. The ease of geographical reach and the voracity of content sharing and creation is vast, and although there may well be "bigger problems" or more immediate concerns for school educators and families that may be equally dangerous in different ways, we want children to be able to explore social media and similar network development, but, if they go too far, and have their eyes and minds glued to Instagram, TikTok, X, and other social media sites, they have no attention left for learning in the real world.

This is a place where parental engagement is vital, including in dialogues they have with educators. We want to be generous when we give children some ownership over where they're exploring and which ideas, theories, and learning mechanisms they're using. That "freedom" or "generosity," however, must have limits.

When Disaster Hits, It Hits Children Hardest

The most challenging time to sustain quality learning is, of course, when disaster strikes.

COVID-19 isn't an acronym that still strikes terror in the hearts of humanity, but the disaster that COVID-19 policies created should. Lives were lost, businesses were shattered, many more individual lives were negatively affected, and many still deal with those effects. But, in my opinion, there were particularly significant negative impacts in "classroom" environments. With that, we lost the ability for many educators to observe and interact with students, and vice versa. Our cornerstone capacity to help children was nullified. In fact, as I speak to children, they almost feel labeled as "the COVID-19 generation." I understand the temptation, but, as I've spoken to many about it, I've come to believe that we're giving too many labels to people. We do this naturally, "Oh, that was the year my parents passed away," or "That was when my career took a sharp left turn." It's perfectly natural to key on life-altering events.

In motion pictures, there are plot points, moments where the story takes a major turn, for better or for worse. Life also has plot points—defining moments, some of which will disrupt education. Rather than letting such moments be excuses by focusing on what we lost, we should reframe them by focusing on what we didn't expect to learn and how we can adapt to meet those challenges, should they arise again.

Learning Loss & Flexible Curricula

COVID-19 is the boogeyman of disasters these days, but the lockdown was far from the only notable catastrophe. From 2021 to 2024, three major storms hit England. They caused only seven deaths, but each took out power for over 1 million people and cost millions in damage, lost wages, and lost school days. In America, Hurricane Helene struck the eastern United States, leveling whole towns and counties. Months later, fires exploded across Los Angeles, California, damaging or destroying thousands of homes, businesses, and civic structures.

In all those cases and many others, cleanup and repairs took months and cost, in total, many billions.

We speak of "learning loss" because that is the educational terminology that was thrown at everybody in the sector during COVID-19 and continues to be used. Survival was our priority, and, right or wrong, education took a back seat.

In a curriculum-based, classroom-centered system, when the school is closed, children really do lose educational opportunities. Montessori education, however, can move forward because students absorb all experiences in diverse ways. We take whatever opportunities arise to explore. Sometimes, there are physical limitations on what we can do and where we can go, but we deal with these as well.

Learning opportunities need not be lost in a Montessori system because they aren't tightly scheduled. They are paused, reworked, or postponed until a more suitable moment comes. Instead, we have many accounts of parents and families learning more with their youngsters than they ever guessed they could. "We make do or do without," is an old saying. Classroom-oriented families must do without when they're without a classroom. If, however, our mindset is plugged into faith, which we define here as "the assumption of the possibility," we make do. Whether we're thrust into our living rooms or shelters, we show our natural, human, survive-and-thrive instincts. We figured out how to make it work.

One example from an American associate of mine:

The lockdowns began in mid-March 2020 in his area. In July, he called a friend and said, "Hey, let's go volunteer at the Food Bank." The friend asked why. My associate responded, "Well, have you got anything else to do?" My associate's friend had five children, active in sports, drama, and other activities; all of which had been cancelled.

There was, literally, not much to do. So, they began volunteering on Saturday mornings at food distribution points. When the friend couldn't attend for one week, his wife took his place. When school reopened, the students had a new, public service requirement, so they joined their parents several times. Over the course of four years, every member of that family and several other friends joined that original pair as volunteers.

This was a new learning experience for each of them and a valuable service to people who needed that service. In years to come, all of them will look back on this experience and remember something they never knew that they had never known.

If we can figure out how to turn a mess like COVID-19 into a family-wide learning experience, we can do it anywhere.

Limited Research

In addition to the impact of physical challenges like disaster situations, we are challenged by a lack of factual data. Factual data is a great "proof" of an "effective program." (Lots of quotation marks there, because those words, in this context, are, at best, inadequate.)

There are volumes upon volumes of writings out there about education, but there's never been much about the Montessori Method compared to other pedagogies. That needs to change. We need more research to demonstrate that the Montessori Method is effective and worthwhile. Such research may be difficult to obtain because we keep getting stuck by the same question: "What are you researching against?"

Colleagues may say, "We've got a tool for that. We're going to evaluate practices and determine whether it's 'authentic' or not." We've been through the "authentic" question, and I think they've missed the point because, if they spend an arbitrary amount of time trying to work out exactly what determines "authentic Montessori" by that very action, we've lost the ability for Montessori to be flexible.

If we have just a few students, we do it differently from groups with dozens. "I've got no roof over the school building!" Okay, then, we tarp it over. "We have no building." Okay, then, we find another building or do what we can do under the sun.

All of that is valid, Montessori-inspired practice. There's nothing wrong with it, and those who tell you there is have an agenda that should worry you. Over the last few generations in the United States, the United Kingdom, and elsewhere, schooling has consistently moved from community control to government control and seems to have landed at mostly union control.

Prior to that, it was home-centered, apprenticeship-driven, and it worked. So, do we even need the research to say that it works? I don't think we do. Should we be researching better ways to instruct our children? Certainly, and always! Businesses and universities spend millions researching how to conduct professional training better and be better at classroom teaching. Why shouldn't there be research on how to better conduct the delivery of child-centered approaches?

There's already a huge body of evidence to support our premises. It's anecdotal, not analytical, and the hard sciences always prefer analytical evidence. In their realm of inquiry, they should demand hard facts. Who said that analytical research was the best way to do research among people? Testimonials are an ancient and accepted way to "prove" an event. Maybe it's time to put away test scores and give other measurements the credence they are due.

Last word

> Everyone said it was my marvelous method which gave this ability to children, and everyone was enthusiastic about it. However, it was neither the school nor the method which produced this phenomenon. It was the expression of the power of the small child and it was a revelation of something that had hitherto remained unknown. The important thing was the discovery of the surprising power of the young child...
>
> We must study the profound and mysterious psychology of the little child, observe its development, and find what we can do to help.
>
> —Maria Montessori[15]

---

[15] *The 1946 London Lectures, op. cit.*

Chapter 4
The Solution

First Word

....

Certainly, it is a new task that confronts us, to study and take into account the needs of this absorbent mind. It is to respond to these needs that we say, 'Education must begin at birth'. We must provide the child's psychic powers with the nourishment they require.
—Maria Montessori[16]

....

We Champion Principles over Ritual

Ours is a worldwide message:

The Montessori Method has value for everyone.

That said, our organization understands there are billions of people who don't have access to Montessori, for a variety of reasons. I initially wrote "good reasons," but they aren't good reasons. They are understandable, based on the limits of our technology, society, culture, and other things. However, the recognition that we are limited in what we can do is no excuse for accepting those limitations.

We won't overcome those limitations overnight. They can't change easily for all the reasons we've mentioned, plus others. Resources are limited, misperceptions abound, some doors are closed, and the people with the keys are not willing to open up to us.

---

[16] *Ibid.*

Something else has got to give, and, in this case, that would be us. We need to expand our reach within the limitations of contemporary society. If the full Montessori program is not acceptable to some, then we bring whatever part of the Method is acceptable. We create an opportunity to include some people in some of what Maria Montessori taught, then use that limited acceptance to prove our Method and convince the powers-that-be to invite us into wider participation.

It sounds so easy to put it that way. Well, in theory, the best stuff usually is simple. In practice, it's where it gets challenging, and we fully understand those challenges.

When people are struggling with education, we can enter with guidance, security blankets of reference, and places for mindfulness. If someone doesn't know how to face a new challenge, we can provide our frame of reference and opportunity to seek solutions that our approach might have. There are many routes to success, and we have one of those, a proven path that may open the door to cooperation on other problems.

Maria Montessori wrote extensively about principles, very little about what we'll call "rituals." We have a large written corpus of her thoughts, her research methods, and how she came to her conclusions. The principles in her writings from a century ago have become the basis of our **sustainable Montessori**. The rituals, like the testing done in the UK and the USA, just don't work everywhere. Lectures, which we classify as a ritual, don't work for some students. The careful scheduling of lessons and a standardized curriculum don't work for some students.

In any endeavor, there are universal constants, ideas that are always true and activities that always work.

"Honesty is the best policy" is an example. Unless you're a spy, it's always true.

"Common courtesy" is another, even though, like "common sense," it's become so rare it almost qualifies as a superpower.

As we expand the understanding and adoption of Montessori as a pedagogy, part of the process must be identifying and constantly reinforcing universal constants. These fundamental attitudes make society work.

A Serious Question

What is education for?

- It is, first and foremost, to make society work—education is the bedrock of effective human interaction.
- Through education, we create understanding of the world and the people who inhabit it.
- Understanding breeds acceptance and tolerance of our differences.
- Acceptance and tolerance make a community possible. They smooth out the interactions between people, leading to peace and prosperity.

One example in a Montessori environment is the peace table. It's set up in a classroom because conflict among children is natural. In Montessori, children use the peace table so they learn to settle differences calmly, with due consideration to all sides of a dispute. Sitting at the table, we talk about how you engage with your friends, what polite behavior is, and how to express ourselves politely to each other.

Once again, if they don't learn this principle as children, they're much less likely to learn it as adults. If individuals don't learn it, communities, tribes, countries, and even races can't learn it. These are the types of principles that underlie Montessori, proven principles that we know have a positive effect on society as a whole.

Teaching names, dates, locations, and other "dry" facts does not accomplish that:

> You have to learn why things work on a starship.
> — "Admiral James T. Kirk" (William Shatner)[17]

Why, not just how. Principles must underlie rituals if the rituals are to have real meaning. For example:

In History: We have centuries of men fighting duels over minor or imagined insults. Imagine how many duels (and resulting deaths) could've been avoided if people understood a few correct principles: Courtesy means never knowingly giving offense. Any offense taken should be met with an apology. Every apology should be met with forgiveness. Imagine if countries, as well as men, adopted such a wild concept.

It's been said, "Violence never solved anything." History is clear, that isn't untrue. War (national or personal) has solved a lot of problems. (Sadly, doing so usually creates more problems.) On a few occasions in history, there was no viable alternative, but such occasions are very few and extremely far between. The careful student of history sees that most conflicts, from international wars to family feuds, were started by people or governments greedy for some form of wealth; in reaction to supposed insults; or to oppress others. If the principle, "Live and let live," were firmly planted in the human mind, history would have been much less exciting but much less bloody.

In Science: Francis Crick, James Watson, and Maurice Wilkins shared the Nobel Prize for discovering the double-helix shape of DNA molecules. However, it was a woman, Rosalind Franklin, who did

---

[17] *Star Trek II: The Wrath of Khan*, Screenplay by Jack B. Sowards; story by Harve Bennett and Jack B. Sowards; directed by Nicholas Meyer. Paramount Pictures Corporation, 1982.

the imaging of DNA molecules that led to the discovery. Courtesy, honesty, and honor—principles that many men flaunted as more important than life itself—would've required that she be given her share of credit and fame, but ego and pride pushed those men to claim the credit and the rewards. Discourtesy, one may say, led to theft and fraud, which are still not entirely corrected.

The Nobel Prize is the ultimate honor in many professions (particularly sciences), equal to an Olympic gold medal. A substantial monetary prize was also presented. The awarding of a Nobel Prize is a ritual that grants worldwide notoriety. It creates a permanent notation in public conversation, such as "Nobel Laureate John Doe expressed concern over the direction of this latest research," in a news story. It opens professional opportunities that most people never see. To claim that prize based on the work of another weakens the public trust in what has always been an important ritual in building trust within those professions.

Rituals bind us and help make society work for everybody. It's a universal constant that Maria Montessori used as a foundation stone for her pedagogy. All were bound in simple logic, common sense, and obvious realities. Most little children naturally see these principles working when they're together in #MontessoriMoments, but, like all skills, they need repetition to reinforce those activities into habits. Parents and educators have the best opportunity, as role models, to guide those moments.

Working Partnerships

Gorton Mount Primary School, now Rushbrook Primary Academy School

Located in one of England's most challenging areas, Gorton Mount's community is characterized by high rates of unemployment, crime, and gang membership. Back in 2010, the Headteacher saw the need for change and went far outside the box to make it happen. She later said:

> The school was in a terrible state. I had to remove some teachers and change how the children were treated. Even if it was raining, the doors stayed locked until 8:45 a.m. so parents [ended up] hanging around outside. I opened the doors at 8:00 a.m. and set up a breakfast club for the kids.
> —Carol Powell, previous Headteacher, 2010

Breakfast was the first of many changes. Ms. Powell introduced the Montessori Method to Gorton Mount, with impressive results. The children were encouraged to learn at their own pace and develop under their own steam, and they were encouraged to do things, learning from their mistakes along the way.

Over its first five years (2005–2010), school enrollment increased by nearly a third, and the school exhibited notable improvement in student achievement. In 2009, there was a 20 percent improvement in the results of early-year tests for the first time. These basic skills tests—including the children's ability to build sentences, communicate with other youngsters, and count up to 10—show how well children are doing as they reach the end of the nursery stage of learning. Some of the children began 18 months behind in development when they arrived at the nursery school, but the Office for Standards in Education, Children's Services and Skills (OFSTED), a government inspection bureau, noted that the school made a significant difference in pupils' lives.

The OFSTED assessment also noted that "the child who has received a Montessori education is more independent in thought and action at home as well as school," and "their skills in reading, writing, and math are more advanced than older siblings at the same age."[18]

These improvements were only a beginning, but they may yet assist Gorton Mount's community to combat their crime rates by providing alternatives to the gang problems, teaching saleable skills that will allow the upcoming generation to graduate as sought-after potential employees.

The school (since renamed Rushbrook) is the only public UK primary currently using the Montessori Method. Montessori Global hopes this will encourage more schools as we continue to support Rushbrook teachers in training the next generation of educators.

Home-Start West Somerset

One of the most important principles in Montessori Global Education continues to be putting children and young families at the heart of everything we do.

Home-Start West Somerset is part of the Home-Start UK federation, which provides support to around 78,900 children from over 43,000 families annually. Many young families struggle to deal with the challenges as new children create changes more quickly than some are able to handle on their own. Beginning in 2023, Montessori Global Education offered its interactive study program to the Home-Start West Somerset team. Learners were given a dedicated tutor, space for guided reflection, and support in identifying how to put their learning into practice. The team now applies a Montessori approach to several Home-Start programs, including Baby Start.

---

[18] Adapted from Richard Garner, "The School that Turned to Montessori to Beat Gangs," *The Independent*. London: Independent Digital News & Media Ltd, 12 March 2010. https://www.independent.co.uk/news/education/education-news/the-school-that-turned-to-montessori-to-beat-gangs-1920114.html, accessed 17 February 2025.

Focused on supporting these families—the babies, their parents, and caregivers—the Home-Start teams provide essential guidance, reassurance and confidence-building opportunities where families need it most—in homes, in local communities and within support networks. Parents and caregivers leave the program with a new understanding of how early education works.

Among other things, new parents learn that if they sing to their infants, they come away with enhanced language skills. If they read to them, the children acquire a love of books, an enhanced vocabulary, and a stronger attachment to their parents. The Baby-Start program involves trust, respect, and following the child through all their activities as Maria Montessori would've wanted it—baby-led. We want infants to explore. Additionally, each session allows time for parents to reflect on what we've done in sessions, what happens at home, and their overall family culture.

> If you were to ask me what the main focus of the Baby-Start program is, I would tell you, it is so families come away from their six weeks of sessions with their babies, feeling like they are competent first educators.
> —Hayley Williams, Family Support Coordinator
> Home Start West Somerset, UK[19]

We Set Priorities, Teaching the Most Necessary Skills

In discussing impact, we all take it for granted that we haven't had time to teach everything to children. This is the fundamental idea behind our hope to inspire a self-directed lifelong learning program by individuals. This limit demands that we set priorities among skill

---

[19] Adapted from "Home-Start West Somerset," *Montessori-GlobalEducation.org*. London: Montessori Global Education, 2020–2025. https://montessori-globaleducation.org/what-we-do/projects-innovations/home-start-west-somerset/, accessed 17 February 2025.

sets and the allocation of resources to teach them. There has always been much debate over what "the essentials" are. I believe that one rises quickly to the top.

There's an immense difference between knowing historical events and being able to intelligently discuss the causes and effects of those events. The names and dates require nothing but memorization, while the debate requires understanding the context: What was going on during those years? How did those events affect other events? How do they continue to affect us today? Can you explain your reasoning?

The ability to discover and understand facts, then evaluate and express opinions based on those facts, rather than speak from a purely emotional response or "gut reaction," used to be called rhetoric and elocution. Anyone who watches politics sees them both in action. Those skills, so intertwined as to be, effectively, one skill, are necessary in a free society, where opinions differ and the community makes decisions. That said, how many schools in the Americas, Europe or elsewhere in the world still teach these skills?

Among our premises is a core idea that we must observe and evaluate the individual student to assess their specific needs. This is a natural extension of understanding and evaluating our community history.

It would be best, we repeat, if the students could tell us what they want and need at any given moment. We also want them to feel that their voices are heard and proper attention paid. Is it not, therefore, vital that we teach them to communicate effectively as we focus on trying to kickstart, to inspire, to start this educational experience right from the beginning?

Obviously, younger children have limited communication capabilities, but we've already warned against selling them short in their ability to do complex things. It's been said that you don't really understand a subject until you can explain it to someone else. Children can and do understand more than we give them credit for. They can and do explain to their friends and playmates how to do things. They are developing communication skills that are priorities in the Montessori Method. Student-to-student, student-to-teacher and student-to-parent interactions are keys to achieving successful child-led learning.

These and other core skill sets will, when children become adults, be cornerstones of their success.

We Deal with Challenging Situations

The flexibility of the Montessori Method allows education to continue in challenging situations.

We touched on some work we've done in the disrupted situations forced on us by the COVID-19 lockdowns. Another example is Petrinja, Croatia, a small town hit by a 6.4 magnitude earthquake on 29 December 2020. The quake caused complete destruction of half the buildings—homes, schools, churches, and community centers and varying damage to the rest. From all over the world, humanitarian aid was received. However, aid workers could only stay for a limited time. "When humanitarian aid corridors left the town, we stayed in silence," said Nadja Matesic, Head of Association IKS, a group founded to support the postwar recovery and strengthening of that community. "Someone had to break that silence," she continued, "and someone did. We just had to look in the right direction, the one where the children are."

Maria Montessori wrote, "The child is both a hope and a promise for mankind."[20]

---

[20] Maria Montessori (translated by Helen R. Lane), *Education and Peace*. Washington DC: Henry Regnery Co., 1972.

Nadja continued, "I believe that every individual who lives near a child is very lucky because children, no matter what their reality looks like, find a way to play, to be cheerful, to sing, to laugh, and to feel. It is their essential need. It is their right." It is also an invitation, and Montessori Global Education was able to help them financially to find a place where the Association IKS could spend time with children and provide guidance on how their team could approach their situation effectively. Despite the trauma the team members suffered because of the earthquake, the Montessori approach has given them hope that they can impact this community in positive ways that will continue for generations.

Since the earthquake, Association IKS has reached more than 6,000 children and families with humanitarian aid, mental health counseling, and education. While accomplishing many small miracles in these lives, Montessori Global Education provided training and mentorship—tools the team could implement in their daily lives, and some ways to review and improve their programs.

Nadja concludes, "And besides the financial part, of course, I think one of the most valuable things that we received is also emotional support and the understanding that somebody actually recognizes what we do and helps us guide it in a better way to give and provide more quality for our community, but also, for our team from the inside."

While rebuilding their town, the Association IKS team successfully completed Montessori training, achieving STAR accreditation.

If we're going to continue to effectively educate children in such a scenario, we have to think and act differently. Montessori Global Education continues to seek out and identify transformative educational solutions capable of providing effective change, even in the most challenging situations.

Children have shorter attention spans than adults, which in this case, could be a positive. Traumas are distracting, and distracted students are not learning. Our educational activities can distract them from their troubles for a while, allowing them to focus on learning instead of the disaster that's momentarily ruined their lives. We recognize that educators and staff members need to be on high alert because, at any moment, any child could suffer a little flashback. That child's emotions could take over, and they could just fall apart.

In such a scenario (which I have never faced and which 90 percent of us will never experience), young ones just get overloaded far more easily than adults. In those scenarios, we can use this distraction as therapy. It can become an entry into that child's psyche. When children are victims of crime, advocates and counselors often just give them a piece of paper and some crayons. Where they are unwilling to talk about what happened to them, they'll often draw it directly or symbolically. Left on their own, children may recreate the house they used to live in or the dog they lost—moments that overwhelmed them.

This is something that needs to be cautiously or mindfully handled because we want them to continue drawing without feeling we're intruding on their privacy or pushing them to do something they don't want to do.

It's a tough call, but handled correctly, art therapy becomes a valuable part of the whole observation route. We can see, in their artwork, that they're distracted from the world around them and focused on that piece of paper. Then, they draw what's important to them, what's on their mind. They probably tend to fantasize about those things a bit. In many cases, they draw it symbolically, but they're aware of whatever disaster is surrounding them, be it crime or COVID-19 or an earthquake. At the same time, they're distracted from the reality of expressing their feelings or thoughts on the subject, which gives parents and educators valuable insight into how they need to deal with that child.

Art therapies—drawing, sculpting with clay, even performing—any form of expression can be cathartic for the child as well as useful for the observers while helping children face and overcome challenging situations.

Too often, when disaster strikes, schools close. Some closures are brief, just long enough to get essential repairs completed. Other closures are permanent because the schools have been reduced to rubble. We want children back in the learning environment with all possible speed, and part of the reason for our haste is continuity, while another part is getting them focused on learning and off the disaster.

Remember, Maria Montessori began her work among children in asylums and similar facilities. She wanted them out and in the mainstream of life whenever possible. Montessori educators don't require school buildings and shelves full of textbooks or other resources. Those are useful, but not essential. The Montessori Method just needs children and people willing to help them.

We Celebrate Journeys of Self-Discovery

An early years educator once told me how empowering it was to see her group of young learners move up and travel forwards to their next year's classroom and class teacher - she felt like she had "done her job," as these little individuals graduated from their very first early years exposure and experience with her, confidently taking on new positions in a new year group and new environment; but as soon as they were walking one way away from her room, another group were walking in for the very first time, and she had no time for reminiscing, sadness or wondering; she had a new job in hand, with a sea of eager new faces to engage right from their very first meeting. This is true across all of education, but especially in early childhood, where the incoming and outgoing scenarios and developmental journeys have been so significant for families and children.

This is why we stress situational awareness and understanding of the child as an individual. We let the children drift, for lack of a better word, from activity to activity; in fact, we encourage it. When they drift, they've seen something that interests them, and they want to experience it. This is self-directed learning and an opportunity for an educator to observe, guide, and assist the child along their journey.

For example, some time ago, my son was in a group where the educator presented several blocks (long, numbered blocks) to assist children in learning to visualize and count. In theory, a child could lay them out in the right height order and learn about counting. Someone else tried to present those blocks to my son. For a time, my son engaged the educator about what to do, and the educator was great with him, suggesting, "You know, we'll make a maze."

So, he went about fitting them together in a small square made up of blocks. As they started doing that, they took their shoes off and walked around, my son becoming more engaged. As it got towards the end of that build, he saw some little push cars. He took the push cars and announced, "It's now a car garage." He took the maze he'd been building and realized it could have another use. He parked the cars in the building, stopped thinking about the math, exercised a touch of tuition and used his creativity to build a car garage instead of something like a cookie factory.

And why not? He's learned for himself something he can do. It pleased him to build a garage for the push cars. Perhaps there's an architect in the making in that little boy's head. Maybe experiences like this will encourage him to learn how to engineer another space station. He's already certain he's going to build an arc reactor. He's convinced of it. For the moment, he's clearly paved his way toward engineering.

It reminds me of a line frequently repeated in a Clint Eastwood movie. He played an old sergeant teaching a group of young, inexperienced marines how to stay alive in a war zone. The line is "Improvise, adapt, overcome."[21] In other words, think out of the box. My son perceived a need that wasn't on the teacher's mind at that moment. He took the initiative to work on that problem. He solved the problem, and the cars had their garage.

It was a #MontessoriMoment.

We Seek Youth Advocates

In that same *Star Trek* movie, Admiral Kirk says to a young lieutenant, "We learn by doing."[22] Some always figure it out quickly, others take time. A friend of mine feels like he never really "learned" to read. For him, it just came naturally.

In a similar scenario, an educator once tried to teach my son how to pour water into a cup to get a drink. She presented him with a tray on which sat a small jug of water and a cup. Before she could finish explaining, my son gently pulled the tray from her, "I'll show you how," he said, not following what she'd explained because he understood the task at hand. He poured the water into the cup, said thanks, and gave the jug back to her. Then, he reached for the cup and had a drink because why else do you pour water in a cup? Then, he sat there with a big smile on his face.

I sat there and thought, "That feels completely normal to me." I knew right then that some in Montessori training would've deemed this exercise a failure somehow because it didn't go exactly as planned; this wasn't the expected outcome. They did not engage. The teacher did not guide.

---

[21] *Heartbreak Ridge*, written by James Carabatsos, Dennis Hackin & Joseph Stinson, directed by Clint Eastwood. Malpaso Productions and Warner Bros., 1986.
[22] *Star Trek II: The Wrath of Khan, op cit.*

Well, technically, something did go wrong. That experience wasn't a replica of a previous experience. That teacher tried to instruct my child on something he already knew, something I have a problem with. Children aren't stupid (despite the way they sometimes act); they know how to do things and they know that they know. They're thinking something like, "I've been seeing people drink since I was zero," was going through my son's head, "So, why do you have to teach me?"

Children are amazing individuals; we dare not underestimate them. They won't buy into a system that underestimates them or abuses them, as current public schools do by locking them into a curriculum and learning mode that they are not biologically designed to follow.

Last word

> If we truly consider education to be the development of latent possibilities, rather than using the word education, we should adopt another: cultivation. The educator must cultivate the potentialities existing in the child, so they may develop and expand. It is essential to take advantage of this highly sensitive period in the life of the human being if, indeed, humanity is to improve.
>
> —Maria Montessori[23]

---

[23] *Citizen of the World, op. cit.*

Part 3
Build Montessori Skills

Chapter 5
The Problem

First word

If we wish to be the interpreter of the child, we must realize that we are studying an unconscious phenomenon. Before consciousness arrives, there is great activity and work in the unconscious. The child is unconscious but has great ability and power.
—Maria Montessori[24]

Note: Today, we might say "a lack of awareness" phenomenon in place of "an unconscious" phenomenon. Children are clearly conscious, but they need time to become aware of their surroundings, and as they become more aware, they interact more.

Why Aren't Children Heard?

It's unrealistic to ask an educator to individually listen to the voices of 30-plus children every moment of every day so they can make decisions on what to do for and with each child. Teachers simply don't have that much time.

That's not to say that we should avoid the challenge. When we talk about the benefits of individualized learning, it doesn't mean that we always want them to learn individually. They'll be part of society as a whole and of other smaller groups. Our children need to learn

---

[24] *The 1946 London Lectures*, op. cit.

how to operate effectively in a community, to work in groups, to collaborate, and so on.

The guidance element that the educator brings to the mix is a fine balance between trying to engage all the voices and trying to be there for everybody while giving them legitimate experiences of real life. So, the child-focusing task, in practical terms, allows the individual's plans to appear gradually and organically. It is to recognize that there are many different ways to absorb the voice of each child. It's not (and cannot be) everybody sitting down and asking the child, "What do you need?" with the teacher listening and putting that child's feedback into a pot to mix with all the other children.

Do children have enough understanding to answer that question in a meaningful sense? Yes, but generally, not verbally. They will show you what they need if you can read the language. The other stakeholders in education—parents, administrators, regulators, and the public at large— also have languages that differ in significant ways. Our goal is to learn those languages and forge a real connection among those stakeholders.

By the way, those individual plans are not completely individual. If we designed a perfectly individualized plan for each child, there would be enough overlap among children that group activities would be valuable, legitimate, cost-saving, and instructive.

How Do We Do It?

In one recent example, an arts-oriented class, the leaders provided access to "real art" as inspiration: A selection of working artists came in to mentor, inspire, and engage with the children. The children were given the tools and the freedom to be in the craft room (or whatever a specific school calls it) and let their creativity fly. Whatever medium they chose, they seem to understand, right from the outset, that this is about expressing themselves to the world through art and feeling heard about what they were doing, whatever that was.

We did this some time ago and approached it from a consent perspective. When we began, we asked if they would like their work to be shown in a global gallery online. We asked things like, "Which project are you happy about sharing? What's more, an expression of your feelings and thoughts that you want to keep private?" That way, they began the project knowing their work might be seen publicly.

We're regularly involved as partners in many student-centered projects. In some, we challenge educators to be less rigid, more open. We encourage them to try something new, instead of teaching according to some curriculum that (as we've discussed before) has been handed down by powers that be without any "consumer input," if I may put it so.

Our challenge, as those who lead education, becomes creating a situation where natural interaction, engagement, and motivational strategies create options that the children see and desire. We, the educators, then promote the activities that yield practical successes, and we toss the other stuff. (If it doesn't meet our needs, why bother doing it?) We're having some success with this project; however, even at the start, we had to question the reality of trying to do this without the voices of children.

Why don't we just include them in things? Because it's actually hard to do. It takes a lot of thought, facilitation and planning. I think we miss a trick if we don't recognize these difficulties. It's an important part of the reason people flippantly say, "Of course, I include the voice of children." I don't think they should do it flippantly; it does take a lot of time and effort. Now, if parents, the community, and society start talking to children, when the children are very young, about what they want to learn, then the child learns that their voice matters and will be integrated into the teaching and how that can make a difference in their education.

There are many challenges with groups of children at school; many reasons child-focused learning can't easily be managed in a semi-sensible way. Children don't know how to regulate themselves in that space. Children want attention; they're used to getting a lot more from their parents than they can get from their teachers. A classroom can become a commotion situation as 30 little people shout and raise their hands to participate. Personally, I want classrooms like this. A classroom with a bit of controlled chaos means children want to be part of what's going on. It's only chaotic because they haven't learned the nuances of negotiation. That's something most of us learn by doing, and I can't see a downside in them learning it young.

Part of this learning to negotiate for attention is listening, actually absorbing somebody else's thoughts and comparing them to your own. Youngsters can do this, and they can blend those thoughts into a collaborative process. We start this in the home, it's in our family from day one—things like "taking turns" and "sharing time." These are necessary skills for young children if they want to have a good relationship with each other. Translating these into the classroom becomes a much more co-created experience as children listen to the educators and other children from the very earliest stages. They speak, they hear, they think, and, most importantly, they feel valued in that conversation.

Mechanism

Children don't naturally know how to do this. It must be taught. To teach it, we have to redesign our curricula. (There are some things that the children absolutely must learn, so I doubt we'll ever entirely escape having a curriculum. The trick is how to present and accomplish what it needs to accomplish.) Teachers have to instruct them to properly add their voices to a conversation, then mentor them into choosing things, or guide them into choosing things. At the end of the year, if we've met our goal, we've covered all the

The Problem

essential information the regulators require, and we've done it so that the children have truly been involved.

This is a whole new classroom, a new kind of classroom experience. It's not simply sitting down with the children and saying, "What do you want to do?" If people want children's voices to be included, they'll fail if they simply say, "Listen to children." We must establish an actual, effective mechanism by which we observe and mentor the children to give us useful information. Without that, I don't think we're helping to solve the problem.

We need to recognize this abstract problem and the practical problem in making it work. First, parents need to be taught how to teach their children to effectively negotiate and communicate their wants. This is the instruction part. Second, teachers have to encourage children to actually do that. This is the mentoring and practicum part. Sadly, among both parents and teachers, there's a lack of understanding of how to take this forward most effectively.

I believe we need to alter two attitudes concerning this whole idea: timing and importance.

The timing needs to be from day one, the day parents bring a child home from the hospital. This isn't something that can start at a certain stage; it's got to be drip-fed through everything. Children can't understand "negotiation" as a concept, but they can choose: "Do you want to sleep with your teddy or your lion?" "Do you want to sleep with your red blankey or your blue blankey?" Understanding that we, individually, have choices is the beginning of understanding how we make choices in a group.

The important issue can be a problem. In some households, parents don't value what small children have to say and, therefore, don't listen to them. When one of those children comes to a classroom, they're at a terrible disadvantage. Even so, we (society as a whole) must value those skills so much that we do whatever is necessary to make negotiation—and, by extension, consideration for others—among our top educational priorities.

I've mentioned the worldwide discussions and consensus that we are suffering a recruitment and retention crisis in teaching. There's also a widespread belief that children are lacking school readiness. For example, there's a potentially global issue brewing around what has become a serious practical problem in some places—massive numbers of children starting school unable to toilet themselves.

(To be clear, that discussion doesn't include infant/toddler care facilities or nursery environments, where toilet training is part of the experience and landscape of development. This discussion refers to the older grades.)

The absence of this skill (and others) means a huge waste of teachers' time because they now have to teach those fundamental skills. The COVID-19 lockdown is being blamed for much of this, but those excuses are growing very old. Children entering school now (2025) were born about the time COVID-19 struck—the lockdowns eased long before they were old enough to be affected by them. We now have plenty of time for toilet training and other things in need. If we're talking about school readiness, we need a value shift because we're discussing skills children need to learn before they get to elementary school. We simply can't waste precious resources on this sort of issue.

(And, not to be tactless, but, returning to the toilet issue, do any teachers want to deal with 10 or 12 of their charges wearing nappies? Absolutely not! We don't pay them enough as it is.)

Am I proposing a fundamental redesign of the entire childhood experience? Yes, and in the long run, I think parents' and teachers' lives would be easier. When children want to engage, they understand when adults listen to them. They recognize engagement. (I repeat, they crave attention.) As part of the decision-making process, we wouldn't get this, "Oh, why are we doing that now?" that we so often hear from today's children.

They want to know what's going on. That's why the principle of Montessori, titled "vertical grouping," works; children don't like the person next to them being able to do exciting things that they struggle to do. A part of them want to get this task done quickly so they can move on to that task. Once again, it's the idea that children can support each other, and all of them gain confidence when they do. I honestly believe the only way to reach this dream will be to expend the effort required and redesign both classrooms and attitudes.

All of this talk of redesign should sound a bit odd, as vertical grouping is a proven, successful model. In the American "Old West" of the late 19th Century, many communities were very small, and the "one-room schoolhouse" was the norm. Older children helped teach their younger counterparts. Even today, older collegians, generally called teaching assistants, teach first- and second-year classes. It is expected.

But the selling point, for lack of a better term, for this whole redesign of the childhood experience is the fact that, ultimately, it will be easier for parents and teachers to help the children along their educational path, or, perhaps, "their educational transition" is the better phrase.

The Challenge of Diversity

The Common Conception of Diversity

Diversity is challenging. It requires effort, time, and resources to accommodate the vast differences among students. That, of course, is the cornerstone of the Montessori Method, but that doesn't mean it's going to be easy in every case.

The first problem is one of definition. In common usage, particularly in reference to society as a whole, it refers to the diversity of race, language, culture, and so on, that poses challenges to a smooth-running community. This is particularly relevant among groups that hope to retain their distinct cultures when they emigrate. Those challenges needn't be mentioned here; they're displayed every night on the news.

But it goes deeper, far deeper: Children, even if culturally homogenous, are diverse. In preparing this manuscript, I spoke with a colleague who is a high-functioning autistic. According to published sources, autism was first identified around 1910, but the psychology community only began widespread discussions in the 1950s and '60s. My colleague attended public school in the 1960s and '70s. School personnel, even the school psychologist, literally did not know the extent of his problems and couldn't offer any effective assistance to help him deal with his situation. As a result, primary and secondary schools were a 12-year, nonstop, horrible experience for him.

We do recognize the vastly different definitions of "inclusion" and notions of "welcoming diversity" present globally today. We also recognize that some reactions—tantrums, disruptions, isolation, even exclusion—are real. They must be recognized and dealt with on an individual basis. These challenges lead to a significant number of students leaving school early in the best-case scenario. In the worst case, young people end up without access to effective schooling.

The Reality of Diversity

Fifty years later, we give lip service to some sort of vague solution, but clearly, we still have the challenges of 30-plus children squashed into one classroom, some of whom have distinct and serious learning challenges. With worldwide teacher shortages, that's not likely to change in the next decade.

There are programs in place to bring specialists in to support educators and, when needed, to assist learners with specific needs, to create a time and space where they can more fully engage their learning style. It's an excellent step forward (where such programs are offered) and should allow greater integration into the mainstream classroom experience.

We want to give all students, including those with additional or specific learning needs, special educational needs, or assistance with disabilities, as much support as we can so they can enjoy the fullest educational experience possible. We want them to have the same opportunities as mainstream students and to take part in as many of those opportunities as they choose to engage.

This should become a cornerstone of our pedagogy, but we have to be realistic about the practical limitations of things. We have only so much working time, we have directives, and we'll never be able to give every student all the attention they need and deserve. In short, we strive for perfection, but we do the best we can and hope it's enough.

We also need the administrators, school boards and regulators to create situations that allow the teachers to confidently tackle those things and say. "Let's deal with this in a professional, realistic, reasonable manner. Let's create practical solutions by being pragmatic about the support that's available within our situation. Let's make it work in a very tangible way because life doesn't stop while we solve these problems. Children still need to experience life and be educated in every moment of the day."

A friend told me a funny story about classrooms. When he was in high school, he had a class with six boys named David. One day, the class was particularly rowdy, and one of the Davids was slouched in his chair in the front row, chatting to the student next to him. The teacher tired quickly of the commotion and leaned over her desk, pointed at slouching David and said, "Hey, David, quiet!"

The room went dead silent.

For about three seconds, then everybody (the teacher included) burst out laughing.

That said, let's fictionalize the scenario: Instead of simply being too chatty, suppose these "Davids" were the students needing special attention to learn the material. The class of 30 teenagers meets daily for 40 minutes, or 200 minutes per week. That gave the teacher just six minutes per student of weekly individual attention on average. Most of the 30 didn't need much individual attention, but these "Davids" needed much more. How does the teacher keep 24 students busy with something useful while she focuses on those six? Is it fair to even do so, and, if she can't, what happens to the "Davids"?

Just as silencing the six Davids silenced a class of 30, a few students needing extra help can grind the smooth flow of teaching to a halt. That's a key point to keep in mind. We have an equal obligation to all 30 students. Do we (can we?) provide additional tutoring for those few after school or during study periods? Can they keep up with the others? If they have to spend a week in the regular class and a second week in added tutoring, and they do this on several subjects, how far behind might they get? How frustrated will they get? Will this lead to behavioral problems?

There are many questions, and the universal answers are non-existent because, at the same time, the teachers are required to teach several standardized information packages to prepare the students for the final exams, which form a large part of their final grade.

In such a situation, which is the norm, teachers cannot completely individualize instruction.

The Diversity of Everyday Life

Firm answers still elude us because these are, still, somewhat new questions. At Montessori Global, these are core questions that we're determined to answer.

Partly, we lack time for perfect individualism. Partly, our mandate includes preparing children to work in groups and be part of communities. In some respects, that's easy because children naturally play together unless separated by adults. However, working together to achieve a common goal is different. We've understood this for decades, and we've designed some experiences, such as chemistry or physics labs, workshops, auto shops, and the like, where students have to work together to succeed.

There's also a movement among some educators to bring real life into the classroom. A rocket scientist, for example, might come into a classroom to discuss all the skill sets that go into getting a rocket into space. The chemist needs to create fuels that generate enough power. Engineers need to design a rocket strong enough to support vastly different levels of varying stresses. Mechanics need to put together what the engineers design. Mathematicians need to calculate launch times and orbits. Pilots need to steer the spacecraft to where it needs to be. Sailors need to pick the capsule up after splashdown. Doctors need to make sure the astronauts are fit before and after flights.

This is a completely different aspect of diversity that needs to be part of the discussion. Students' individual talents and interests are diverse. Those need to be channeled into cooperative ventures.

If We Don't Listen, We Can't Accommodate Diverse Views

One Size Doesn't Fit All

In the world of understanding, in the dialogue of trying to question and challenge, we frown upon assumptions. In research, people are not allowed to make assumptions because that cannot lead to evidence-based decision-making. Unfortunately, in the real world, people make quick-fire assessments without context. Those are assumptions.

For example, we assume all the students are in a good place each day. In effect, we say, "You can all happily take this test today because you all feel well, you're all happy, and ready to enjoy the test."

No. What about the one in the corner with anxiety? What about those who need special assessment assistance, such as the dyslexic student who needs more time to read and comprehend the questions? Sadly, in my experience of talking to long-standing educators and students reflecting on their own learning experiences as a "labeled dyslexic," giving them more time to complete the test is actually giving them more time to sit there and panic. More time can't help them because they can't formulate what they want to put on the page.

Giving them an extra 20 minutes to sit in an awful environment, and they just wind themselves up even more and more about not getting the work done, is not useful. So, we end up with assumptions being put into a lot of these scenarios, assumptions that don't allow for variation, adaptation, alternative, or personalization—any of the words we use to leverage this idea. It leads us back to one of Maria Montessori's original premises. You learn about your students, then evaluate them by observation.

What about the excellent student with ADHD, for example? He sits down in a math class to take a test, and his brain freezes up. He looks at the page and sees the questions. He's demonstrated his knowledge of the material in previous classes, but at that moment, he can't remember anything about the concepts being tested. He can't answer a single question. He fails the test, and had it not been for excellent work on other assignments and tests, he might've failed the class. (This is a bit of an extreme example, but not entirely unrealistic.)

Under the modern curriculum-based scenario, he was scheduled for a test. Was it his job to be ready? Yes, of course, because he knew it would happen. What if he didn't perform? Well, then, he failed, and it counts against his semester-long performance.

Fortunately, in forward-thinking situations, many educational establishments around the world are now set up to provide recognition of circumstances when there's a documented situation. Individuals with specific learning needs (mental or physical) are given allowances to assist them in dealing with challenges. It's about recognizing that this person needs A, this person needs B, this person needs C; therefore, each needs to be given the opportunity to work at the level appropriate to them. This gives them the confidence to do the expected work while getting a fair assessment.

In their formative years, adolescents deal with a lot of things. We, the adults, don't understand how much of their out-of-school life comes with them into the classroom on a daily basis and (for lack of a better term) intrudes into everything they do. This seems weird because each of us was an adolescent back in the day. Adolescent problems shouldn't be hard to grasp, but we can't understand their experience because we never understood it when it happened to us! Adolescents can't compartmentalize experiences and save them for later study and evaluation. Adults can "leave it at the door," while younger, less experienced people can't. So, some of them get labeled as problems and, unfortunately, those labels might stay with people long after a school term ends.

Adolescents (and younger children more so) often experience things that put them on the slippery slope toward not achieving their best work at all times—for example, my seven-year-old plays county-level tennis. On one particular day, he and another boy were practicing doubles play, and my son over-reached. He should've let the other boy return the ball, but he's seven and got overexcited. The other boy shouted at him, "That was my ball, you shouldn't have taken my ball." A normal child's reaction. My little chap looked at him and thought, *It's not worth me arguing with you,* and he simply disengaged from the game. He kept playing, but without his full attention or enthusiasm.

Even though this was a coaching session, we (the coach and parents) always hope that our children play their best. This shows us how their skill levels are developing, and parents always hope their child is going to win! (Part of being a parent is living, a little, through your children's successes.)

In that moment, though, if the coach compared my son to his partner, who was still all-in on that game, he might've judged both boys without understanding that one of them was regulating his emotions well and the other wasn't. That coach, then, might've judged my son's result instead of his effort.

If these were pro players, and my son had a problem with a partner, this adult, professional son would say to himself, "Okay, later, we're going to talk about this, but for now, I need to focus on the game. I have to perform well. We need to win this to move on in the tournament because we get paid more for winning more." He could compartmentalize the situation and schedule a time when some reaction is appropriate. This childhood incident could've been part of the ongoing process to develop that adult, professional partnership, but on that day, my son didn't handle it like an adult; he handled it like the seven-year-old that he was.

Assessments, as they are now, would've focused entirely on whether my son won or lost; on how many points he scored versus how many points his partner scored; on how many points he successfully returned, and so on. Assessments need to be able to focus, or at least take note of, how my son was feeling at the time, and how that affected his game. We're a long way from that day.

I think we've got some intense focus on this type of assessment right now, and we need to highlight where and give those people due recognition for their effort to ask the right questions. The conventional wisdom is very different. Many don't want to acknowledge that such problems exist because that suggests they caused the problems or couldn't solve the problem, and they, thereby, lose face.

Just today (as I'm writing this), the UK Department of Education gave out more statements about how our new government won't (supposedly) allow any failing schools because failing schools fail children. I'm tempted to think they mean the building is at fault here. Are those revered, "ivy-covered" walls somehow failing children?

That's completely the wrong rhetoric. The problem is the management. We haven't managed the school system well enough. They, the bureaucrats, are not getting it. Either they don't see it, or they see it and refuse to acknowledge it.

A Metaphor

Curriculum schools are cookie factories. (I've mentioned this before.) They churn out millions of biscuits daily. We want schools that are sit-down restaurants, where each customer orders a steak and mashed potatoes or fish and a side salad or whatever suits their fancy that day. Now, I can pick up an adequate meal for a few quid at a fast-food place, but it only barely qualifies as adequate. If I want a meal that really satisfies and has high nutritional value, I'll have to sit, waiting, while they cook an individual meal, while I spend four or five times the amount of money to sit in a room with "atmosphere." And that, of course, is the sticking point: It's all about money.

Which leads to another point: Not every educator is a master of many situations, just like those in the kitchen. Some create masterpieces with a cow and a potato; others take a fish and astound; some specialize in ethnic or regional cuisine. That is, some are capable fast-food fryers, while a few dazzle with taste and presentation of the highest quality. Each has their place, and if our metaphorical restaurant is to succeed, we can't simply let them do their thing. The right cook needs to be in the right kitchen, for their sake as well as the customers'.

This leads to a completely different but closely related problem: Clearly, there are places around the world that have yet to open decent sit-down restaurants. They're lucky to have a couple of decent places serving good home cooking or a few fast-food eateries. If, however, they all started working towards that place of culinary delights, sharing the costs and pooling resources, it could work. It's worked well for chains and franchise owners in many industries. If people, on a large scale, buy into the idea, it won't cost as much as they're imagining to create bigger, better schools.

But, even when governments are enthusiastic supporters, they alone aren't enough. We still need families to prepare their children for the formal school experience, and to support and guide teachers on how they deal with their children's individual needs. In such cases, education has already started before the children step into a classroom. When parents share the responsibility, especially for those most basic skills that we mentioned before, educators have the freedom to actually pursue the pedagogy they were trained in and are more motivated to do the things that made them want to do education as a career.

Even adopting every money-saving method available, the program still costs money, sometimes, a lot of it, where significant improvements are needed. That, in particular, is where the power of grassroots efforts is demonstrated. If the people support it, the government must get voted out. That's why I want Montessori Global to focus our efforts on change from the bottom up, as a grassroots effort. Then, as momentum builds, some people in power will start listening because they'll make that mental shift. They may even come to champion the Montessori Method. At that point, we begin to have the influence we need to make significant changes.

Lack of Peer Engagement or Formal Interaction

There are those who firmly believe that you cannot change the system from the outside. Political, social, educational, whatever it may be, effective change must come from within, gain acceptance, and, ultimately, absorb all other ways of doing things. If that theory is true (and, perhaps, even if it's not), Montessori has difficulties engaging with the education sector as a whole. Most educators are curriculum-bound, generically trained and what some term "non-Montessori" educators, viewed as outsiders, not part of the "system."

A similar problem exists with the public. The word "alternative" is frequently used to describe Montessori, even though we have never claimed it at all. As a quick reference point, we often hear people say, "Oh, I've heard of Montessori. It's that alternative education school," or other, similar language. We used to hang on to that description, because we are **the** alternative, but people think of us as **an** alternative. I think that's far too subtle for most people to grasp, so we are not trying to nuance anybody's understanding of us. We're now trying to be clear and definitive in our language about who we are and what we do.

Every country is different in its approach to education, and some people have been under the same sort of system for a very long time. Certainly, in the UK, and I don't think the USA is vastly different, my generation never thought that change could happen as rapidly as it has happened in recent years. Everyone who is paying attention knows that, in just four years, change came and (in a literal moment) things were significantly different as new leaders took office. When governments change dramatically, as they have recently in the UK and USA, new leaders can shake things up very quickly, but you'll always see backlash against that from "the Establishment" (those who've traditionally held sway politically. Often, new leaders act in public to get headlines, to set their agenda, or just to show off the power they now have. Whatever that might do for political purposes, it doesn't do anything effective for education.

In education, the establishment is immensely powerful because (a) they have power over our children and everyone knows it; (b) we want the best for the children, and (c) they are, in theory, the ones delivering that "best." If we're going to change that, we need to convince a lot of people to make a change.

There will be some colleagues who disagree with me, but we're back to this idea of our testimonials, case studies, and impact assessments based on those contextual pieces. It's not the comparative hard data like test scores and reading evaluations that are simple to understand, but lack context.

Our data is context-rich. We don't compare city situations, where everyone has similar opportunities, to remote or rural regions, where some children haven't been to school before age five or six. We try things, we see what works and what doesn't and go from there. That's how we begin to mobilize our momentum.

We mobilize, and I know this directly, parents as an emerging new voice. Also, we, as a movement, haven't spoken enough to that earliest part of the educational system, to educators in training. We haven't made them a part of the discussion. That, too, is changing. These are new areas for us, but we're intent on making those audiences aware of what we hope to do. We want them to fully understand the Montessori Method, how it's delivered, and what it can deliver for every child.

We see educators as a group to whom we've never fully opened the door before now. We know that educators all over the world are seeking better ways to do their jobs, because that's what good people do. So, we hope to be something better than what they're seeking. We don't want them in their own homes at night, tearing their hair out, marking till midnight, stressing over reports and grade cards and still trying to teach the next morning. I see us becoming the go-to place they seek out for support and guidance.

We are, however, time-poor. We can't slow down the delivery of educational content, due to the demanding nature of our curriculum requirements. While all this revitalizing goes on, we still have classrooms full of children to be taught.

Standardized Evaluation Is Possible Only When All Parties Agree

When do you evaluate students?

In discussing evaluations with a colleague, he mentioned that, when he was in school, there were three basic divisions—elementary school (K through grade 5), middle school (grades 6 through 8), and high school (grades 9 through 12). (These, of course, vary from place to place.) He recalls numerous evaluations—quizzes, tests, and occasional special exams to evaluate job prospects, college entry, or other things. He asked me if there were key points along the path, such as the transitions into kindergarten, into middle school, into high school, for example, which can answer the vital question, "Does this student have the skill set to continue and succeed?" It's an idea worth considering, tests that form a baseline assessment that could assist teachers in designing individual teaching programs.

I agree with the principle. To a point, all those quizzes and tests have value; they're formative, a process for teacher feedback. But I believe we need to be more creative than we have been. We have to acknowledge that students learn at different rates, putting limits on the value of across-the-board testing. I also think teachers, as well as students, need to take ownership of the complete process, using these transitional moments to test both student competence and teacher effectiveness. Teachers should also perform regular peer assessments, observing each other in the classrooms, testing teachers' ability to connect with students.

And those touch points or transitions my colleague identified are reasonably uniform, give or take a year. Whatever age a system chooses, there are definite stepping off points. There's much to be said for the term "readiness." In this case, it's about readiness for the next phase of their lives. Wherever these transition points are set, we've got to develop and maintain an extensive (dare I suggest, universal?) confidence that whoever reads the evaluations will do so in an atmosphere where the expectations on all sides are the same.

How do they get on the same page? All the people involved need to approach evaluation from the same perspective. They need to hold a pre-conversation with co-creative expectations. They set a standard which has scale, spectrum, and range—a standard that we're all cognizant of and willing to accept.

And therein lies the difficulty: The more narrow those moments get and the more externally verifiable those moments are, the less they replicate real life because people have such wide varieties among them. In addition to having standards that are, in fact, standard across the board, we also need people who are qualified to create, administer, and interpret these assessments.

"Heaven forbid," some would say, "that we give this power to the teachers." Instead, I say, "How amazing that would be." Well, even among teachers, we have wide variations that cause challenges. I had some teachers who were completely there, enthusiastically wanting students to excel. Then, there were teachers who desperately wanted students to do well on tests because that reflected well on them and their profession. And, of course, the few who (even more than the students) desperately waited for the closing bell. It would be a challenge to find and professionally train enough people to administer the test we're discussing.

I'm part of a peer network where I assess professionally for the educational sector. There is a self-regulation process in the teacher-educator community. There will always be some who want the quick win. There are also some who want to do the due diligence and do it well and uphold the respectability and dignity of our profession. There will always be variations in between, but I fundamentally believe in the profession and the work we do. I support my colleagues and the power to be found in allowing educators to be a professional movement and to self-regulate.

But show me a scenario where teachers are actually left to do that. I don't see them. They've got all sorts of administrators, business managers and other so-called leaders to deal with. As much as we want and need better evaluation practices, as a matter of professional survival, pleasing those non-educators generally takes precedence over developing and implementing a better system for our children.

It's an old question, and I'm not certain we're closing in on the answer that we need.

Co-creation

Here's a question for you: How can children fix the problems that are now inherent in our system of educating them? In a word already mentioned, co-creation. We've not yet sufficiently discussed the co-creation of learning experiences. Children's voices in the process are important because, as we've said more than once, they're the ones getting educated, and they're in the best position to tell us how to most effectively teach them. Unfortunately, the idea of listening to children gives some people this absolute knee-jerk reaction against giving children too much freedom and power.

In some people's minds, simply suggesting that we listen to children causes incredulous responses like, "What do children know?" and "How do they know what to suggest if we haven't given them parameters, and so on?"

Well, there's a saying in America, "Corporate boards sometimes make decisions that are so stupid, no five-year-old would make them. Sadly, you never have a five-year-old in a corporate boardroom when you need one."

A serious intent meets a humorous presentation, but we look again at how Maria Montessori saw the educator's significant role in providing boundaries. She didn't disparage boundaries; she advocated for freedom within limits.

Regrettably, we still deal with many who are not yet willing to listen. Hopefully, "co-creating things with your children" is better, a meaning more palatable to the average citizen or school administrator, than suggesting "freedom within limits." It sounds a little bit less harsh to some ears. I think we can achieve the goals of co-creation—getting the voices of children into the discussion through facilitated opportunities. It will be a challenge to sit down with a child who's in first grade or second grade and ask them, "What do you want to learn today?" or, worse, "What do you want to learn this year?"

Do children of five, six or seven even have a concept of a year? We'll need to keep our creativity open. If I take a group of preschool or reception/first graders out into the open with our wellies on, my observation skills will see that child A is looking at the sky, wondering: "Why is the sky blue? Why do the clouds float and move? What's going on up there?" Meanwhile, child B looks straight at the dirt and digs around to see what kind of bugs live down there. Then there's child C, whose whole intent is grossing everybody out with some snake or toad she's caught.

When we come in, someone goes for a book, another for paints or clay, to and still another for the building blocks.

It is a wonderful thing to watch the children engaging in things that truly interest them. But even with as much freedom as the children can handle, a classroom can't become a free-for-all. We want, as part of this co-creation process, teachers who are able to put a group of children (not a class, a group) into a stimulus-rich environment; rich in options both numerically and categorically. We want to see what toys they choose. Each of the students, based on individual preferences, will be drawn to something in that environment. We want them to create something. We care less about what they create; we're intently curious to see where they're drawn. When they choose something on their own, I think we've found something they care about, and we can build on that.

We can be empathetic educators, a facilitator instead of a lecturer; the person who's willing to do the work in support of that process and keep opportunities flowing. That will involve mediating conflicts now and then if two or three children want the same resources at a given moment. We want them to know they have free access to resources, but also that accessibility is not universal and unlimited. We want to teach them that resources are limited. They want everything when they want it. Sometimes, they're going to have to share or they're going to have to wait. Sometimes, they're even going to have to ask.

Which raises a new set of questions: How do we assess and evaluate the acquisition of skills like patience, sharing, courtesy and manners?

That could be the subject of another whole book.

Last word

> Clearly, we have a social duty towards this future man, this man who exists as a silhouette around the child, a duty towards this man of tomorrow. Perhaps a great future leader or a great genius is with us, and his power will come from the power of the child he is today. This is the vision which we must have.
> —Maria Montessori[25]

---

[25] *The 1946 London Lectures, op cit.*

Chapter 6

The Solution

First word

> *We can only help man if we aid the child to be better adapted to the future of civilization.*
> *—Maria Montessori[26]*

Advisory Panels and Evaluation Processes

Some time ago, I met a single mother who thought, "This is the end." She was divorced, unprepared for an ill-timed pregnancy, and convinced she would struggle through life with her baby. She had no real hope for something better for her child. She didn't even know what options she had. She started going to classes and building her self-confidence. After a time, she could say to her domineering former mother-in-law with a firm, "That's not the way I want to do it." She even went so far as to declare, "This is my home."

She took control of a bad situation and made herself capable. When her child became a toddler, they joined a toddler support group, and she eventually started volunteering within the group. She had come full circle.

She now wants to continue volunteering and helping other people like herself. That doesn't sound like much, but it's a transformational attitude. When I consider the potential benefits and impact of advisory panels, we need to pull this kind of knowledge together—

---

[26] *The 1946 London Lectures, op. cit.*

actual experience with our Method with actual people and real-world results. I think we have a duty to hear what might be called organically orientated testimonials, stories that matter, which we first heard out in the community, among practitioners, parents, and others.

We don't discourage or reject laboratory research, evidence-based inquiry, or the results, which are useful. We do, however, take that research in the context where it's found. Experimental data is not a day-to-day life experience that a single parent can pick up and run with; they'd get no value from it. A laboratory evaluation has to compare two similar items. We're not so similar to traditional education that most comparisons are useful.

For example, researchers make sweeping statements based on studies of five-year-olds tested in September and again in January. They're trying to answer the question, "How does their literacy change over these months?" It's a valid question, but incomplete if you simply take a random group of children and look at how well they read.

These findings take no notice of everything else that's going on in those children's lives. Things happened during those months, some good, some bad, some, on occasion, spectacular or catastrophic. These affect children's learning. When we deal with their reading skills in isolation, we ignore the fact that children's lives and activities are very much not isolated. I simply can't fathom how that's permissible in so many academic circles. All evidence-based studies suffer from this deficit. Fortunately, the good researchers admit this flaw, but so many of them don't.

Experimental studies simply don't have as much value for our purposes as empirical (anecdotal) studies. Even though, in the common mind, it's the other way around. We are used to getting and analyzing facts and statistics—tangible proof. That doesn't work so well as we develop individualized education practices. Individuals are not quantifiable

The Solution

because you can't quantify every factor that affects us at any given moment, much less over a long time.

Right now, we're working on a project called Voices of Children. It's experience-based and I'm keen that the mentors involved in the project understand that they must be aware of other influencing factors involved in the children's lives and, on occasion, need to dig deep to find and deal with them.

Back to my seven-year-old's tennis game. My lad mentally disengaged from that game. I could see he was still playing, occasionally hitting the ball, but in his mind, he'd quit. He wasn't in that game anymore, and, on the drive home, I said, "I saw what happened today. Tell me about it."

He said, "Well, he upset me, and I wasn't going to help him anymore."

"Okay," I replied, "so we have a reason why you're not helping him, but you're a pair, you're a team. I get that things can influence the way that you play, but I want you to think about something else."

I explained that, if someone other than Mum had been watching him play at that moment and didn't understand any of the context—that he's just seven and still negotiating his own emotions—they wouldn't have understood his reaction to things. They might've looked at his play and thought, "Well, he hasn't got the technique there. He's not extending; not doing other things." They would've made assumptions based on just what they saw today because they have no context: They didn't see all his good work on other days. They didn't understand what he was feeling right then. The context was so rich with his emotional regulation going on, trying to sort himself out, hating that he couldn't do everything in one moment. His game suffered as a result.

That's the problem we deal with when analyzing and assessing people. We assess in the moment, but we're not one size fits all. We must be alert to context all the time: spelling tests, the odd pop quiz, any of it. Whatever's going on at home could really have an effect on each person all the time, and we don't give them a chance if we put them (in our minds) all in the same scenario and assume that they should all have the same outcome.

Engagement and Encouragement in Co-creation

Most of you have probably heard of the "impostor syndrome." It's more common among women, but it also happens to men. One common example: A woman is appointed to the board of directors of a corporation. She walks into the board room for the first time and sees perhaps a dozen to two dozen men and two or three other women. She begins to wonder, "What am I doing here? Am I really qualified?"

That's a trap. When you enter a high-level position, it isn't because you have a pleasant personality. In the boardroom scenario, you were elected by shareholders, stockholders, trustees or appointed by the owner. Why? Because they trusted you to do the job. The fact that you were invited into the room is a statement that you are qualified.

We don't have that option. The single parent mentioned at the outset of this chapter qualified herself to do a hard job—motherhood—and volunteered to help others learn what she had learned. That's powerful, but not always enough. Suppose she applies for a job at a nursery or school. Will they accept her experience and desire to help as a qualification? Some will, some won't.

Certification

There is something valuable about documentation. Almost every industry, trade, and profession has some certification program, an industrywide set of standards that demonstrate an individual is capable of doing a job correctly.

It allows one to ask, "I've done this successfully, I'm one of 'those people,' are you one of 'those people'?" It creates a community in which we can engage with a starting place of common understanding. As a community with a baseline set of goals, we can better engage and encourage co-creation because we're all heading toward the same end result.

We don't do this exclusively for those who are fully qualified and well-experienced, those educators with 20 or 30 or more years in classrooms. We do this to recognize those people who are making an effort to change children's lives and trying to apply Montessori practices as individuals and parents like that single mother.

We also do this so that other people, those who are not acquainted with the Method, will respect and acknowledge the practitioners as qualified. It's evidence that the education establishment, which prides itself on its many certifications, will subconsciously accept it as a qualifying factor. One that sets in people's minds the fact that you are serious about this and have been professionally trained so that you really do know what you're doing. You value education enough to set your standards as high as ours and prepare yourself to meet them.

Networks & Online Communities

Completing training and earning certifications creates networking opportunities. Opportunities create dialogue. Dialogue encourages co-creation. We are, after all, a charity that doesn't have unlimited resources, particularly because we don't charge for much of our training. Among my hopes for Montessori Global is that we always have a suite of completely free training modules.

We have one program that's completely free at the moment. There are costs for other programs that we frequently pay or subsidize for access. Our suite of free modules is our demonstration that we uphold our charitable mission to disseminate the Montessori Method to everybody who wants it.

If we could get everybody that we've ever spoken to, or a large majority of them, to sign up for the free programs, a forum or network naturally forms, if they have an online place to do so. They can then post things and suggestions to this group of like-minded people. If we can build such a network and create an easy access point, similar to social media sites, two things will happen: First, I will have a chance for a direct audience, should we wish to sell into it for something in the future. Second, and more importantly, it gives us a chance to strengthen that group. As we make our strategic collaborations global, we can say to them, "This is the network that we're bringing with us," and "This is what we're bringing to the network."

Both Montessori Global and the participants benefit. It's not crass to suggest we might make available some discount cards or other group benefits. Many do that as a membership benefit, and the groups receive funding if members sign up for those offers. That funding is vital to some of those groups. In our case, it will support our free programs. More importantly, we'll have hundreds, then thousands and, perhaps, someday, millions of collaborators—using the programs, suggesting new programs to meet new needs or adding the experiences of all our collaborators, allowing us to improve programs in ways our core group here in the UK might never see.

In addition to connections we can generate internally, there are numerous organizations around the world that could become valuable partners. For instance, the Chartered College for Teaching in the UK is recognized; they're a Chartered organization run by Dame Alison Peacock, a veteran of more than 30 years in teaching, professional teacher training, and as an author. For almost 200 years, this teacher-founded group has promoted teaching as a profession. The current objects of the college (as revised in 2017) are "the promotion of sound learning and the improvement and recognition of the art, science and practice of teaching for the public benefit."

Both organizations will benefit from a proactive cooperation that creates an upward pathway. This is, in fact, "Montessori in business"—the "collegiate" relationships that can be formed within and across sectors to recognize that Montessori principles are both relevant and reliable in many contexts. It is vital in such scenarios, however, to remain alert to the necessity of organizational alignment and shared vision. We feel we have that with The Chartered College for Teaching. It is clear, transparent, and gives purpose to our cross-promotional activity.

After all, children are keen to know the purpose, as are our communities, leading to understanding and insight and "buy-in" where needed. If benefits are not obvious and forthcoming, children aren't shy about making their displeasure known. All you have to do is pay attention to their physical reactions. Once they become verbal, they'll usually describe, with considerable enthusiasm, what they like and dislike if the teacher (or anyone else) learns the right questions to ask!

Individualizing Outcomes

Also described as "charting solo progression" or "measuring the immeasurable," I've toyed with this idea for a while in terms of a landscape. In landscaping, you're trying to look at a wide variety of flowers, shrubs, and trees and fitting them all into a cohesive vision. We're trying to articulate that, and in mixing many things, we can create something uniquely beautiful.

An effective landscape does not have a single focal point. Our attention is drawn to many different elements and aspects of the home situation. On a personal level, I've been thinking about it as "creating a landscape of educational opportunities," one in which there will be something for everyone.

This contrasts with the orientation of farm products. Farms generally have a cash crop, be it wheat, corn, milk, beef, whatever. The smart farmer also cultivates other crops—hay to feed the cows or vegetables to feed the family—but those don't get equal attention with the cash crop.

Likewise, the desired outcomes of landscapes and farms are vastly different. The farmer is after a profit, while the homeowner desires to come home to pleasant, relaxing surroundings. Curriculum-based teaching is like farming, always focused on results. Montessori-based teaching focuses on creating an atmosphere in which children can reach out and fulfill any one of many outcomes.

How Children Can Assist in Evaluation and Engagement

In the classroom, curriculum-focused education is all about judging the output and answers from the test, based on preconceived notions of the test creators, whereas competency-focused education keys evaluations on skills and how well students do things. It doesn't key so much on what students produce; it's about creating a method for them to obtain whatever their desired result is.

Figuring out what they desire is a remarkably simple question. Children evaluate everything they do, subconsciously. When a friend comes to visit, they run into their arms. When a favorite food is on their plate, they can't get enough of it. If a school program meets their needs, that is, what they think their needs are, they need no coaxing to participate. But their feedback in these moments, and those that come later upon further personal reflection, are vital. They are often opportunities for emotion-filled gems of "feed-forward" material, material and guidance that educators need to guide the next steps in individual learning journeys.

The Solution

This is often "unspoken," however. Children and learners are often unaware of the impact that their feedback and evaluation processes can have on their subsequent learning experiences—and I'd suggest, that's fine. It's the way it should be - subtle and unassuming, but natural and integrated in true, holistic learning and teaching in practice.

Last word

> So, there are two plans: one is to disseminate knowledge, to follow a syllabus. The other is to look to the life of man and serve it, and in serving it, help humanity... We must give him the means and encourage him. 'Courage, my dear, courage! You are a new man that must adapt to this new world. Go on triumphantly. I am here to help you.' This kind of encouragement is instinctive in those who love children.
> —Maria Montessori[27]

---

[27] *The 1946 London Lectures, op.cit.*

Part 4
Make Children Visible and Their Voices Vital in Their Education

Chapter 7
The Problem

First Word

> When I say that we must take the child as our teacher you will probably object, saying we must educate the child and give him all sorts of information, that he must learn the subjects we think important. Do not have these prejudices. When his energies are freed, the child will be better able to learn than before... This child who stands before us with his marvelous hidden energies must lead our efforts. When we say that the child is our teacher, we mean that we must take his revelations as our guide. Our starting point must be the revelation of the characteristics of the human individual.
> —Maria Montessori[28]

Why Are Stakeholders at Odds?

We must clarify "stakeholders." We're looking at two camps here: First, decision-makers—those in charge of things, such as administrators, funders, and politicians. Second, practitioners are people who have extensive day-to-day experience in education, such as teachers, researchers, professors, Montessori-trained people, and, of course, parents and students.

---

[28] *The 1946 London Lectures, op cit.*

Vision

We could establish parents and students as a third group, but we differentiate the groups in this way because parents must stand with the hands-on classroom educators. Parents should be educators for their children, and their children have extensive experience with the results of the classroom experience. They should have more contact with educators than with any of the others. Like educators, they live and breathe the education experience on a daily basis.

I'd even go a little bit further to say there is a divide between the camps. The first believe they are (somehow) the visionaries; that their issues, concerns and considerations are worthy of guiding the final decisions because they can see the bigger picture. They think that they're the ones who are safeguarding the workforce and citizens of tomorrow. They're looking at that holistic view. But that definition of "holistic" doesn't suit them. It doesn't fit because the holistic view lies in the everyday experience, a place that they (as children or parents) may have resided in, but one which does not impact their primary tasks or responsibilities as decision-makers.

For those not aware, the funders are a special subgroup within decision-makers. We've got a half-dozen different types of academies and multi-academy trusts, as well as all sorts of business arrangements with local authorities. In some cases, they own and operate the schools. In others, local districts own the building but sub-contract the running of the school to others. There's also a full range of businesses or connections that run schools. Their definition of "holistic" will differ from ours because they're in the business of education, while education, for us, is a passion.

(I know what you're thinking, "Oh, heavens, the bookkeeping!" You're not far off.)

Now, I don't want to put words in their mouths. This first camp might not even use the word "holistic" at all, might not even recognize this concept. But my sense is that they believe the vision they're striving for is somehow holistic in terms of the future outlook.

When talking about decision-makers, their definition of "holistic" would naturally be different from ours. Let's take politicians as an example. If I'm a member of Parliament (an "MP"), I look at the whole of the United Kingdom of Great Britain and Northern Ireland with a view toward the need to graduate competent, skilled, mature, adult people who will contribute to our economy and our community. That, to me, is "holistic." When talking to, from, or about the perspective of the practitioner camp, I see "holistic" as focused on the individual and their total educational experience. Both are legitimate points of view, but they do not overlap as much as we'd like.

In recent years, it's become obvious that the decision-maker camp has been saying they've got their finger "on the pulse"; that they know what's required to fix education for tomorrow. They recognize the need to provide a better developmental strategy for kindness, for worthy citizens, and for people who have the social and emotional skills to connect with other people. They're only just realizing that these have been pulled out of the curricula and need to be returned. However, they say, "We're putting it back into the curriculum. Here's how we're going to teach it. Here are the subjects. This will be our focus."

Meanwhile, the practitioner camp is living it. We're trying to draw the community together through life experiences, through a variety of opportunities exploring each other's strengths, through actual physical community. In short, their "holistic" view creates a unified curriculum, while ours creates a unified experience. Today, the practitioner camp has a defining opportunity to say, "Our vision differs from the decision-makers. They claim they understand it, but they don't see what's actually happening right now."

We worry that decision-makers will completely take over education, break down all the components that have proven successful in educating our students to become capable, confident human beings, and start separating out what has worked so well for us, replacing it with some theoretical model that's never been tested or proven.

I'm excited about this and, maybe, fixated a little too much. If so, it's because I see their definition of holistic (whether they use that word or not) based on a set of desires, goals, and needs that differ dramatically from ours. If I'm right in that conclusion, there's going to be a portion of what they do and what we do that never overlaps.

We understand that both camps have different obligations. MPs, for example, are elected in more-or-less five-year cycles. That means businesses and school administrators must deal with changes (some of them drastic) in public policy that accompany changes in government, and with the politicians' need to cater to the changing opinions of their electorate. Meanwhile, decision-makers obligate themselves, to a point, to certain actions based on their interpretation of quantitative analyses like reading or math scores. As we've mentioned already, an MP or business leader can easily sell favorable scores to constituents or the board of directors as "proof" of the success of their policies.

We answer to different constituencies—the parents and the students—with different standards and expectations. We try to teach curiosity, critical thinking, self-reliance, and other demonstrable but not easily quantifiable life skills. We also obligate ourselves to evaluations, but even our assessments are very qualitative in nature. At the same time, our analyses must be sold to parents because each set of parents will choose whether or not to send their child to us based on our sales pitch.

The Pitch and the Plans

The idea that these different visions are fueled by different obligations and goals is no surprise. Even when Maria Montessori began her professional career, over 100 years ago, there was what would today be called the "educational establishment." She created an alternative to that existing program, and that alternative was founded on a significantly different vision for education. The debate as to which is the better vision continues and will continue in the foreseeable future.

Today, as a global organization, we meet with a range of different responses and levels of interest to our "pitch" for enrollment. When we start these conversations, we begin with the research we've collected, which includes looking at projects that are innovative in particular parts of the world.

We get interesting reactions. We're often facing, if I may put it so, a blank slate—people who know nothing of Maria Montessori or the Montessori Method. We're suggesting something new and different that we hope will fit their views of and goals for education within their cultural norms. From all I've seen, it's really important for us to have researched what we call "ages and stages"—their readiness for change. We need to recognize the educational backdrop of that culture; what it has been and continues to be, and, therefore, their capacity to receive messages like ours, then accept and adopt them.

We have some projects that are already operating in what we'll call "rural" regions that have had to live with limited educational options. Some of those projects, for example, give young girls access to modern education where it has not been available. That's a huge line in the sand and a huge step forward for some because that community traditionally has young girls being home-schooled, with priorities for the home and caring, taking precedence over any wider worldly educational experiences. Their culture may expect them to marry young and create a new family and a home at an early age, and they need specific skills training to be successful. That cultural imperative isn't going to change soon; therefore, initiatives "on the ground" and in the community become essential. In some countries, this is a community hub setup / pop-up style with weekly sessions to attend; in others, we can highlight initiatives such as "Montessori-on-Wheels." In this example, a Montessori-equipped bus comes around to neighborhoods, providing additional education on the doorstep. Without it, many young girls simply aren't allowed to take part in education outside of the home. We hope these examples demonstrate that additional education is valuable for these young women, changing attitudes over time to show that an in-school education can provide the skills training they've been getting, plus more that will enhance their family life. That's one mode of recognizing a need and filling in places while respecting their traditions and culture.

Of course, reactions to ideas like this vary. Some places enthusiastically welcome such initiatives, while in others, projects face opposition or a lack of interest. Some of it is because of the simple fact that some of these projects did not originate in-country. This was a story we had heard before.

For many years, our training college has offered people outside the UK the opportunity to come to London for residential tutoring. When I joined the organization, having evaluated this model, I proposed that there was a new problem emerging: people couldn't afford to come on their own and often couldn't get sponsorship from their government to come to London. That group included much of Latin America, Sub-Saharan Africa and large parts of Asia. What we thought was working really well for the best part of 15 years now faced situations where it didn't work. And, by the way, it wasn't just the money. Our model also needed to recognize potential cultural differences that, for many potential students, felt like a barrier to access and success when they returned home from a "UK-centric" delivery experience. We also started to realize that there was much more work to be done to prevent a Western idea of Montessori being passed on, that didn't always fit into a wider culture.

Cultural Expectations / Societal Norms

It's an ongoing discussion: What's best for **them**?

I had, once upon a time, a conversation with an educator who got it. I think she had her finger on the pulse of her regional community. I think she understood what they needed. We got into a really detailed chat about what she wanted to offer in her training. One interesting detail came from that exchange.

As you know, effective teaching touches everyday living. Part of our chat revolved around musical instruments. She said she'd need to find X amount of dollars to buy a specific type of musical instrument from Europe. I asked why she wanted that particular item. That was shown in the materials and training programs, was the reply. I asked more about what might be more accessible locally; why would a European object be necessary? If there was something else locally, why wouldn't they use that? I shouldn't have been surprised, but that hadn't occurred to her—Montessori training does appear to "look" a certain way. I had assumed that she would personalize her takeaways from her training and unlock the opportunity for alignment to resources that were culturally relevant, and, by the way, there was a man close to her home who made instruments (drums, especially) at very affordable prices. So, she could support a local artisan while making sure the local children saw their teachers using something they saw in their day-to-day activities.

A solid everybody-wins scenario. (I also pointed out that she could have a few drums of other styles, if she wanted them, so she could show her students something from a different country as well.) I was reminded that you don't say you're trying to provide an excellent educational experience if you fail to use what's already on their doorstep; things their grandparents might have used.

That's still a conversation that we have regularly when people say, "You know, you're so different from previous models of training."

Well, yes, and thank you for the compliment. We are striving to be a global organization, which means we're trying to reach a global audience while remaining respectful of and interested in the local culture. How else could our "pitch" be accepted?

When Do We Start Educating?

The "early years education" space starts at different ages and stages, anywhere from two to seven. Families in some parts don't expect their children to participate in any sort of educational experience before that local starting point. They didn't start younger, their grandparents didn't, so that's become a generational cycle that we have to tackle. We want to help people adapt to new possibilities. To do that, we have to start where they are, with programs they're comfortable with.

We have our vision for now, and we have a vision for five years down the road, but ultimately, we need a generational vision. We need the people just now emerging into adulthood to understand the Method before they have children, before they start wanting things for their children. This way, when they want something different, we can help bring the next generation through our program as a normal part of life. Their children then grow up thinking, "I'll keep doing this when I'm a parent because it did so much for me." That's the generational attitude change that we're trying to message. It's not a quick win, to be sure, but it's the only win that creates long-term change and upshift.

By the way, we also run into cultural resistance to the child-led learning concept. Because Montessori has benefited (and suffered) from a high academic reputation over the past few years, we naturally meet those who simply strive for greater academic achievement. We hear, all too often, "Our child will thrive and succeed by going to a Montessori school with its regimented approach."

We, then, try to say no, but our sustainable Montessori succeeds as well because we offer more freedom, which encourages more creativity. Ultimately, we want to hear more voices of children bubbling through, telling us what they want to learn. That doesn't always go over well. "I'm not paying for my child to be directing their own education. They need to be told what to do because that's how we'll attain the best results."

It's another difference in culture and vision which we sometimes overcome and, at other times, we don't.

The Babysitter Classroom

Another point to be consideredis that pressure on the system rarely gets discussed and has nothing to do with children or education. The "babysitter classroom" has arisen so that mothers can get out of the house and go to work. I think this is a huge problem, a difficult spot to put educators in.

This isn't why most people send their children to school, but school has always been a place where you can put children during the day. The COVID-19 lockdowns rammed that home because there was uproar from every part of the globe about how people couldn't cope with their children at home, disrupting their lives. That says something somewhat uncomplimentary about some parents.

That also takes us back to the core definitions of education—what is it, why are we doing it, what goals are we accomplishing? Is it some sort of annoyance that parents are expected to help them learn to read? Is it an imposition to expect parents to prepare their children for going to a public school? To toilet train them? To accustom them to sharing and cooperating with others?

This has been going on since World War II. Many women left home to take factory and other jobs while the men went off to war. When the men came home, women were expected to return home and raise the "baby boom" generation. However, women had become unsatisfied with the limited roles society had determined for them. Beginning in the 1950s, many went to work, and the classroom became, partly, a babysitter, though it was rarely called that in public.

As the number of working women rose, the government saw two incomes to tax and got behind the idea. Activists saw the horizon, and the "feminist" movement arose as a political force. Birth rates dropped as America urbanized (and needed fewer children to run the farm), and some began to see children as a distraction to the fight for women's rights. (We take notice of these cultural movements without making a value judgement on any of them, except to say, for some, these changes were a positive; for others, they became a negative. We strive to work with all families to create the best outcome possible.) But children are never a distraction or a necessary evil. They're a privilege to anybody who's ever met one. Our societies don't progress as mothers and fathers abandon their roles as the earliest and primary educators, we regress. We, as a society, have failed our children.

A Reminder

The tone of this book, which we captured and described early, focuses on the commitment to, the responsibility for, and the deep-seated desire of most parents to love their children and seek the best for them.

I think we have to start from that place, knowing that it's not absolutely true for everybody, but I think true enough for the vast majority. We, then, have a common starting point from which we can elevate the conversation around the return of parents to the position of primary caregiver, which includes the earliest and primary educator. Most parents want that responsibility; they want to pass on their belief system and culture to the next generation. We've come away from that old attitude, "children should be seen and not heard," or the ideas that children are a menace, a nuisance, or a distraction or that they're mucking up our lives, hurting our careers, or whatever other falsehoods have been polluting society for the last several years.

You're Not Worthy!

Now, as the balance of power has leaned ever more toward the classroom over the past several decades, attitudes have also changed. As teachers became the primary educators, many have come to believe this is the way it should be and always should have been.

Homeschooling has always been part of the educational landscape, but, as homeschools have increased in number, the education establishment increasingly sees them as a threat to the all-but-total monopoly they have possessed over the raising of children. Homeschooling has exploded, in part, because some parents have begun to see schools more as propaganda machines, churning out indoctrinated *apparatchiks* (Russian, "party operators") than free-thinking, independent adults.

Governments and the education industry have come in to say, "Oh, but you're not qualified." While it's true that parents lack the college graduate's certification and the ensuing state-sponsored license, they emphatically **are** the first educators. To this, the establishment responds, "You want the best for your children, but you can't give it to them. Give them to us for eight hours a day, five days a week, for nine months of the year, and we'll deliver back to you the properly educated child." It's a message that some embrace but others decry.

Almost everyone has now realized that this ongoing contest between the establishment and the family is real. Many parents didn't step up when they should've and, now, they're wondering how it all happened.

In part, that's immaterial. It happened, and now we have to deal with it. By taking parents out of the education equation, by separating home from school in a very distinct way, even with the best of intentions (which we assume professional educators had), from a safeguarding perspective, parents need to reassert their voices, their votes, and their control over their children's education. As we said before, every teacher farms a new crop of students every year. As much as they care about their students, it's a very temporary relationship. Families are forever.

Recognitions

The foregoing is written about the (striving-for-the-ideal) traditional family. We understand, as clearly as everyone else, that there are children who need to be in school for their own safety. There are millions of children around the world for whom home is not a safe environment. The reasons are many and varied, and immaterial at this point. For whatever reason, these children need to be protected, and school might be the safest place in their lives. We encourage and support all efforts to keep children safe in improper situations.

We likewise recognize that schools might be unsafe for some. The "boys-will-be-boys" attitude, and the resulting unrestricted bullying which we've finally come to learn, isn't limited to boys, and must be addressed. Many people are working hard to make sure that school *is* a safe space. Through many challenging times, there have been significant numbers of people who speak of teachers as "the one person who cared about me," or who identified abuse or other dangers and spoke up. That is, the teachers, counselors or other staffers who did not let this child or that child slip through the cracks.

All of this reinforces our basic premise: Children are unique individuals with unique needs, and we (parents and others) must hear their voices regarding their educational and other needs. Many can't speak freely. They need to know they can speak in a protected space to an audience who will listen and act.

Assessment Outcomes Focused on "Recognized" Successes

Obviously, we can't avoid assessments, the powers-that-be demand proof of concept, and rightly so, especially when they're paying the tab. Sometimes, however, the culture becomes too focused on assessments. An educated people should be the desired end, with assessments just a means of measuring progress. However, if good grades become the end, trouble starts.

I used to work for an organization that oversaw examinations and the awarding of ratings, and so on. They had a new operation starting in Asia, and they thought China was the location to be the test, one to be emulated, they hoped. The company's desire for success led to a lot of local freedom in the startup period. When the program manager finally went over to look at the factory that was manufacturing the support resources, the factory management showed off machines, several of which were rolling out answers to exam papers. The manager then declared, "This is how we're going to get high results."

Fraud?

I'd call it a black market in selling the exam results, but it wasn't underground. The selling was completely open and widespread, done precisely so that students would achieve high ratings. They were proudly doing it rather than hiding it away in some back corner. It was literally the complete opposite of how I would have intended to help those students get good grades, and so blatantly done that the images will stay with me forever in the "I Can't Believe My Eyes" folder.

Different Views and Pressures

It reminded me that there are parts of the world where things are done so differently that I can't say we can apply the same names to what they do and what we do. High achievement, in some cultures, is the be-all and end-all of their existence. Japan, you may have heard, has been criticized for effectively brutalizing its children into success. Six hours of school followed by four hours of homework was the norm. They weren't given time to be children. They excelled academically but, as adults, were expected to give the same level of commitment to their employers. Many ended up working themselves to death before age 40. The job, the promotion, the raise—that's what they were educated to do, that's all they know. Life outside work ceased to exist and, sadly, so did many people.

We can do better, and, hopefully, we can convince some of these cultures that a well-rounded life is the better path.

The Art of Observation

We recognize there are differences of opinion. We recognize our difference in the value placed on early education and on children in general.

We promote observation-based education. We had a project in Singapore some time ago. It was an art-based project, and during six weeks of classes, the children were highly creative. When it ended, the children went back to the regimented curriculum common to Singapore's school system. Comments were received: "They had a nice time," "The program outcomes were very impressive," and "They hope to do it again." As a project, it failed in part. The decision-makers did not recognize why it was "impressive"—it succeeded because it was new, exciting material with new methods that engaged and held the children's attention. We didn't want that. We wanted the difference to become the norm, the difference to become the norm, and the difference to become the norm, and we wanted that to become more attractive to parents and administrators. Yet, they chose to stay with the "education establishment."

We get a lot of that in pedagogical circles.

Instead, when educators understand and buy into our concept, they realize that, to get the voice of children and truly lead those young minds, observation becomes the driving force of the classroom. It's a dynamic where the teacher sits back, not at the front, commanding the room. That's visually different to regulators, funders, and other decision-makers. It would be funded differently, evaluated differently, and might start a snowball effect to change the whole face of education.

(Yes, we dream big. Why don't you?)

We recognize the impact and significance that this could have. A friend of mine went to college in America. He told me, "I had some teachers who were exceptionally good lecturers. I remember one particular fellow, a geography teacher. He had his lectures down, and he laid the subject out beautifully. Now, as I was interested in this subject, it was great for me. I could absorb it all, but this was a general education class. He had engineering majors, sociology majors, and art majors, and most of us didn't care. He didn't seem to care either. He gave the lecture; he gave the tests; you passed or you failed. That was the whole class. At that school, we had to take X number of general education classes, so, if you failed, it was your fault; this was what you signed up for."

I'm thinking this is a problem for many teachers in the UK and USA, and elsewhere, I would add, for many who've spent their careers lecturing, but not teaching.

We subscribe to a "flipped" classroom model. When I discuss this around the world, I call it the preferred approach for children, or for any educational person who's trying to engage in their own learning journey. I suggest giving the students the material in advance. Let them absorb it in whichever way they wish to. Let them assimilate information. Let them come up with questions and challenges for a session that the teacher facilitates. That's just a mind-blowing idea to some. But, if one looks to history, it's no more than the world-renowned and universally respected Socratic method.

In the lecture-mode classroom, I've seen so many educators who deliver the material, but they're terrified of a question-and-answer period at the end. They might not say it, but their body language screams, "Don't ask me anything!"

I've trained so many teachers in exactly this scenario. They're petrified by a situation that includes a chance for people to ask questions for which they haven't specifically prepared. Those teachers might be caught, somehow, not knowing the answer to a basic question, which makes them lose face.

Well, quite frankly, that's the wrong way of doing it. Educators must be confident enough to say, "I'm sorry, I don't know the answer offhand. Let's find out together. Let's research it. Let's both learn something on that topic."

That teacher is saying, "Let's co-create. Let's collaborate." How lovely that would be. It would require a high level of self-confidence for an educator to learn from a child/student publicly, but that's the heart of observation—seeing an opportunity to help a child learn how to teach themselves. That's part of the solution.

Expectation to Be "Active / Hands-On"

Have you ever used an old-fashioned hand pump on a water well? Often, you need to "prime the pump," to pour a little water into the pump to help it get started. Lectures can do that, laying some groundwork, introducing the subject, opening up the curious mind, and igniting curiosity:

The common proverb, "Tell me, I forget. Show me, I remember. Involve me, I understand."

The common trade apprenticeship plan: "See it. Do it. Teach it."

Both, and others we might name, are tried and proven formulas for success.

Redefining It

I deliberately use the term "art of observation" because it's an opportunity for teachers to learn what students need. Somehow, the opposite is too often true; we seem to see students coming to school wanting to explore, to do all this stuff, but the system flips them by saying, "You will observe, we will teach," often enough that students believe it.

As the educator, that attitude only allows teachers to see a small part of a student, the bit that sits in a chair. That's not the art of observation. We need to observe a child at free play if we're to know that child. There's a big movement to say that play-based education is what we need to have, and Montessori Global supports that.

If we truly achieve our goals, the art of observation will come to the fore as the preferred professional approach for teaching children.

The Bottom Line

Both in the UK and the USA, we have parent-teacher conferences. They may call it different things, but it's a meeting in which parents and teachers discuss a child's work and how to improve it, if necessary.

Question: Why weren't my children asked to come?

Answer: I don't know or understand.

I think there's nothing that could or should be said about children that they shouldn't hear straight up. If an educator can't handle their presence in a way that is appropriate for that situation, then, I think, we must question the purpose and effectiveness of those meetings. "But," some say, "we don't want to open that whole can of worms." At Montessori, we do! We think their voices are important, but as a society, we aren't listening to them. (I repeat this point to engrave it on your minds.)

We return again to the factory metaphor. Mass production is faster, easier, and cheaper; we all know that. Is childhood education's overarching priority to be cost-effective and simple?

No, the priority is to educate children and support the parents as they prepare their children to be thoughtful, considerate, deliberative, effective, and responsible adults, and to do it in a way that meets that child's individual needs. (That is, it should be.)

Some will say the teachers can represent children's svoices to the regulators and the community, but that's the teacher's interpretation of the child's voice, which is delivered through that teacher's frame of reference. In legal terms, that would be hearsay and inadmissible in court.

In all of our contexts, the child's voice is absent from decision-makers' attention. That is not acceptable, and Montessori Global will be there as champions of including those voices.

Last Word

> The child has the capacity to educate himself, not in typical schools with their exact syllabuses where children must be obedient, but at a school where he is not controlled, does not have to compete, but can work with enthusiasm according to natural laws. If we do not know these laws and respect them, then we are in danger of spoiling this great work of the child's.
> —Maria Montessori[29]

---

[29] *The 1946 London Lectures, op cit.*

Chapter 8

The Solution

First Word

The purpose of education must be to elevate the individual; otherwise, education would be of no use. This must be the goal of education. We must wish to love humanity, instead of merely wanting to apply a preconceived plan.
—Maria Montessori[30]

If all this is going to work, our second camp, the practitioners, needs to initiate a fundamental shift in our core view of education. Then we need to push it to become the predominant attitude, the first camp!

This is our call to action. This is our vision: a world where children are integral to their own education process. While working on this book, I was also furthering the project "Baby Start," which I mentioned earlier. This is a successful community project, but one that can evolve. In "Baby Start," the focus is on families and often on women who feel unprepared to be mothers. As I reflected, I thought that we ought to have a new vision in place for that project, even more focused on the view that parents are their child's first educator. With every angle I look at, that's what I see. As the new mother and father deal with the day-to-day minutia—meals, shopping, laundry, appointments—they can be teaching small lessons. A two-day-old baby won't see it or understand it but, if the parents develop the habit of consistently teaching the child, by the time the child can understand, the idea that

---

[30] *The 1946 London Lectures, op. cit.*

we're constantly learning lessons drawn from the world around us will be normal, as will the confidence of the child in the parents as the primary educators.

Trying to get every parent on the planet to understand, at the same level, the significance of this model will be a multi-decade, possibly multi-generational, task. Well, I don't deal in decades or generations; I deal with now, in what I can lead Montessori Global to do this year, this month, today!

I can start; I can get the ball rolling.

I can get my organization to understand what we're aiming for and set projects in motion that prove the theory valid. That might be all I can do in my term as CEO. Well, as a wise person once said, "All you can do is all you can do." I feel this is of paramount importance, and it feels like something that we have to start on, whatever small scale we can and help it grow.

Promote Learner Voices & Elevate Recognition

In the UK and USA, I see politicians trying to slap plasters on problems, covering them up with fancy rhetoric and short-term solutions they can tout as successes during their next election cycle. As I write this (2025), there are discussions (and some action) about abandoning or dissolving the US Department of Education, revising state inspection bodies and closing various governmentgovernment offices to redistribute funds and responsibilities. The bureaucrats are supposed to be technical experts who assist in making formal education better. Since the politicians took charge, that hasn't happened. Internet articles state that both countries have fallen behind their former leadership in academics at all levels.

The Solution

Neither the voice of the parent, nor the voice of the child, nor the voice of the professional has been able to overcome the voice of the politician here, because the politicians control the purse.

"To do what's best for the children" should be our battle cry. There's hardly a politician who'll disagree (publicly) with such a statement. In fact, they'll (publicly) applaud and agree with you. What they'll do or say privately is a completely different question. Fortunately, if parents do their "due diligence," they'll figure out what politicians are doing and, when reelection time rolls around, will vote for someone else if the actions don't match the rhetoric.

So, the key, as we have discussed, is to create a situation where we are aware of and focused on what is best for each individual child. The answer, in theory, might be as simple as mobilizing parents as voters to rein in these regulators—the elected politicians and those they appoint. Parents need to keep control of the political machine that has all the money and all the power. Their votes are their power base. Parents should not be afraid to fire people when they screw up.

It's a ridiculous idea in many minds, but we do it in other areas of our lives. We fire underperforming employees. Why not in public service?

In every aspect of life, someone has to have the last word; it's called responsibility. In most cases, the law holds parents responsible for their children. That is, parents can be forced to pay if a child damages another's property. In the UK and the USA, children under 18 cannot always travel alone or do many other things without parental permission. So, why should parents as primary educators be such a new and controversial idea?

Refocus on Detailed Research

I often think that the solution is to push pause on some things that are turning, whirring away in the background, but we don't know if they're working. We do see that, while all of that is happening, the goalposts have moved. Situations change every minute, but you know, once somebody does X or Y or Z and has some success, people notice and ask questions.

"How did they do that?"

"Can we get in on this?"

And so on. Unfortunately, we return to, from an educational viewpoint, our ongoing lack of research. The decision-making camp has to justify their continued employment, and therefore, they love data that's easy to read and obvious to interpret and that demonstrates what makes life better.

Real, detailed, effective research doesn't take a week; it takes years. It's easy to say, "Let's decentralize this, let's bring that together, let's put in that approach." Policies, however, which look good on paper, may not look so good if we're talking about what "everybody knows," even though no one's looked at the potential outcomes 20 years down the road. So much of what we're doing is based on what we've always done. That's what creates "conventional wisdom," but conventional wisdom is often not so wise.

A Sustainable Stewardship

It's been said frequently over the last few years, "We are stewards, we inherited this Earth from our parents, we'll pass it on to our children, it's ours to care for, not to use up."

The Solution

Thoughts like that remind us that we're temporary, like the old hiker/camper mantras: "Take nothing but pictures, leave nothing but footprints," and "Leave the site better than when you found it."

We also speak of a "sustainable Montessori," a program that'll outlast us. The workforce of the future will need technical skills based on specific occupations, but they'll also need basic skills like creativity, problem solving, directing their own education, leadership, planning and carrying projects to fulfillment, and a host of others. The Montessori Method is dedicated to instilling those skills from childhood. They aren't talents, available to a select few "born with it." They are skills anyone can develop.

As I've mentioned previously, we have a worldwide teacher shortage. If we're going to fix the problems of education, we're not going to do it in classrooms with a teacher and 60 students or more.

How, then, do we fix that lack of qualified bodies?

Firstly, we don't get so desperate that we say, "Oh, look, you have a pulse. You're hired," then expect them to get qualified. That cheats the children of the education they deserve. We don't advocate that untrained or otherwise unqualified people be "professionalized" by government edict and put into classrooms. Teaching is still a profession (perhaps a vocation?), and classroom teachers require training and preparation. We simply have to review and decide exactly what training they need and how to best provide it. Everybody who understands education disagrees with this wholesale, open-arms approach. We're not going to "dumb it down" or place unqualified people in charge of our children.

But we do need to face the situation and change it, which won't happen overnight. Where would the money come from to make a major investment in recruiting and training? We don't have it in public education. (Private education works differently; they have other options, but they also face challenges.)

There's good news alongside the bad: Not everyone in society does it for the money. Many of us work at something we love doing and are satisfied to earn enough, so we don't need to get rich. We're happy, I dare say, to put up with some problems because, well, every job has them, and "If you love what you do, you'll never work a day in your life." Those are the people we ought to be finding and recruiting. Those people can change how we do things.

For our part, Montessori Global can provide Maria Montessori's method, plus everything we've learned since, as a safety net—a support system, an advocate, a frame of reference that says, "I'm doing it this way because I have over 100 years of evidence telling me it's right." I think we can provide a backbone of support that, hopefully, will help with recruitment and retention.

I'll add that Montessori is comfortable, as a movement, because, unlike many other pedagogies, we have significant experience in being populated by career changers. Many of our graduates come to us from other professions with technical expertise. They come later in life with significant, meaningful, real-world experience. In fact, a significant proportion of the Montessori community comprises people who've had a different career, and many also have children. They've realized that not everything's rosy in the world, and they want better—a desire that ultimately led them to Montessori and a second career.

Their trajectory is steep. They come to us already highly qualified, experienced practitioners in other professions or trades. We'll always have a conversion route—every job has a learning curve—but these transitioning professionals can negotiate that route faster. We're currently operating many projects across the world, staffed by professionals and people who came up through that program and are now teaching or mentoring others.

We see these as real-world oriented, innovative, exciting projects that try to bring in other professionals using a variety of nontraditional roles. In addition to our coaches and mentors, we host guest lecturers—industry leaders who can bring in advice based on the day-to-day realities of a particular industry or a look at the potential future of a sector. They can dialogue with educators or administrators, providing additional experience, insights, and support for school systems. As reimbursement for these contributions, business and industry leaders meet young men and women who might, in the future, be valuable employees.

Educators of the Future

Looking at our future needs, in other sectors as well as in education, I think we need to pay careful attention to how others come into the sector. Those new routes for qualifying experienced people may vary from place to place, but that broad landscape is going to be necessary for us to meet future needs. At the same time, we need to do more to break down the divide between parents in homes and the community.

So, a question naturally arises: if I wanted to teach history, do I get a degree in teaching with a history minor or a degree in history with a teaching minor? In most countries, it can be either, depending on where you want to end up. We already have that flexibility in the system, so we can add more flexibility. Think about this: if we recruit, as a second career, successful nurses to teach health or engineers to teach math, or geologists to teach science, parents are going to respond, "Oh, wow, our children aren't just being taught by professional teachers, they've got real industry experts or sector specialists, too!" We want to broaden the entire concept of accessibility in educational theory.

We're not advocating the perception, "Oh, an excellent engineer must also be an excellent teacher." Instead, we need more, "This excellent engineer now has exceptional training in pedagogy; therefore, she's now able to effectively share her training and experience with my children." That, we feel, is a realistic, attainable goal.

Existing organizations can facilitate career changes at this level, helping those who choose new paths and giving them the mentoring that makes it work. These are great; we approve of and cooperate with some of them. They demonstrate that our theory (which isn't ours alone) works. We're happy to be a leader in this and responsible for a professional practice piece.

Our present system is unlikely to produce the outcomes that will be in demand. We must do it differently.

Promote Observation/Mentoring Among Educators

"Best practices," as they're called, keep changing as we learn more. Some things, however, don't change.

The family unit is fundamental to society. They know each other more intimately than anyone else can. They know how individuals learn, their particular needs, and what suits them. Families are dynamic, watching individual changes and offering encouragement in a supportive atmosphere that encourages growth. All this is possible because you spend more time with your families (those you grew up in and those you create with your spouse and children), meaning you observe them more often and under more varied situations than anyone outside the family.

We can't duplicate the length and breadth of that observation, but we can imitate it. To meet our future needs, especially with people

The Solution

coming into education from other industries, we have to expand our observation of professionals and mentor them constantly over the long-term. They, current and future educators, need to be willing to engage in that observation and mentor themselves if we're to succeed.

Initial success in mentoring is measured by the person being able to do the job autonomously. They've learned the mechanics of self-examination and learned how to analyze their performance and improve it without the necessity of outside observation. Long-term success means they're able to pass on their knowledge and skills to others.

That doesn't mean we leave them on their own once certified. Follow-up observation and consultation reinforce the learning and enhance the educator's ability to analyze and improve their performance. Montessori Global, as a paid service provider, strives to do exactly that. We start with knowing how those people evaluate themselves, and what mechanisms they already have in place. We add our data, our existing observations, and evaluation protocols to create reports that can be used to explain a provider's validity and status or recognition to the administration.

Somebody within the school or district can then look at individual educators or groups of educators and determine whether they meet the local standards. We're very intensive with our observation, and our experience allows us to review and assess in ways that help individuals and schools to create continuing improvement plans. It's a straightforward process of observation and mentoring that answers an important question for educators: "How fast am I progressing within the parameters that I know are expected of me in this or that role?" That is an attitude to be valued in teachers and every other profession or trade.

From a is, the Montessori standpoint, why did we design this program?—It's specifically about the cycle of self-reflection and self-improvement. Our goal is to complete this process with an educational organization and initiate a continual development and improvement program for individuals, schools, or districts. We can cycle through our program again and again and again until we come to a place of individual or organizational ownership over the process; until it becomes second nature. It should be comfortable for anybody to question their actions and their outcomes because, if we can't do it for ourselves, how can we do it for the children? There's a disconnect there, not only from the role model perspective, but also from the facilitator role.

In the USA and the UK, among many other countries, most professions require continuing education credits to maintain current licensing, registration or similar. It is accepted, "welcomed," and not unusual. However, it is not so popular in the education sector. I've challenged colleagues on this. I frequently hear: "We've come up with this, we're coming up with that, we've got some protocols. We're going to see how others do with these, and then we're going to award them something." Alternatively, we hear "I took a qualification, I did what I needed to do—I am already qualified—I am too busy to take on anything else."

Commitment to Continuing Professional Development (CPD) remains a "work in progress."

Maybe, someday, we may figure out a simple, effective way to involve the attitudes of children toward their teachers, too? (Watch this space!)

Last Word

> Teachers should cultivate a staunch belief in their mission. Only then will it be possible to create a new world through education. However, if this highest of aims is to be attained, educational methods must radically change also to become

an active aid to the psychic [i.e., psychological] development of the child, in an environment prepared following dictates culled from exhaustive study and diligent research...

The teacher should possess this same faith [in the child]. In fact, he should become imbued by it so that he may contemplate with the same hope any advance, however slow; so that he may investigate the causes and modify the circumstances that impede or delay the normal development of the children entrusted to his care.

—Maria Montessori[31]

---

[31] *Citizen of the World, op. cit.*

Conclusion

Montessori's Future as an Accessible, Inclusive Model for All

First word

....

We find ourselves at a moment in time in which spiritual life is neglected and materialism is extolled as a virtue; in which the physical prowess of human beings has surpassed that of nature and in which we glimpse the horror of universal destruction. Because of this, we proclaim that the development of creative energies, of the higher characteristics of human beings, is one of the most urgent needs of our social life...

The question is to bring about a radical change in the way we view human relations, endeavoring to influence men's consciousness by giving them new ideals, fighting indifference and incomprehension; to awaken in man's spirit a sense of gratitude towards other men. This can also be done with children. In fact, these endeavors should begin with the children, giving them the opportunity to reflect on the social value of work, on the beauty of labor carried out by others, whereby the common effort enriches the life of all.
    —Maria Montessori[32]

....

---

[32] *Citizen of the World, op. cit.*

Our Goal

The Montessori approach, which places the child at the center of the learning process, naturally fosters creativity, curiosity, independence, and resilience by allowing children to take the lead and providing a holistic environment that addresses their needs. As of 2025, Montessori Global Education has taken bold moves to dedicate time, effort and resources to re-setting the public, global awareness of this educational approach. Their global team are dynamic and forward-looking, promoting the Montessori philosophy, recognizing its ability to nurture a joy in education, a love of learning, exploration, and discovery. These guiding principles have led the organization to its core mission: "To make Montessori available wherever it is needed, anywhere in the world."

—*The CEO Vision*[33]

Meeting Those Goals

To assist educators, we created STAR (Standards, Training, Accreditation, Review), a recognition program. STAR promotes excellence among educational professionals—standards based on those set by Maria Montessori over 100 years ago. STAR recognition requires the highest learning and teaching practices, exemplifying an attitude of innovation and flexibility, all focused on the needs of the individual child. Montessori and STAR reimagine what accessible, high-quality education can look like for communities around the world.

---

[33] Unbylined, "A World Where Every Child Thrives: The Mission and Vision of Montessori Global Education," *TheCEOVision.com*. Lewes, England: The CEO Vision LLC, 2025. https://theceovision.com/a-world-where-every-child-thrives-the-mission-and-vision-of-montessori-global-education/, accessed 19 March 2025.

Conclusion

In addition, we provide continuing education opportunities—access to lifelong learning programs and professional growth pathways which encourage self-reflection. We believe that administrators, regulators, teachers, and everyone else in the education sector need to take a good, hard look at what they're doing, on a regular basis, and ask, "How can I better serve the children?" This "take charge of myself" attitude empowers educators to become decision-makers in planning their career paths and in encouraging children to lead their own educational experience.

A key part of this reflection-enhancement program is Montessori Centre International (MCI), a world leader in providing Montessori training, specifically in early years education. For two-thirds of a century, MCI has had one ambition: to facilitate the development of and access to quality early years teaching.

We've had the privilege of talking with educators all over the world, searching for positive ways to collaborate for the benefit of our children. Currently, we're spearheading a search to identify quality Montessori schools worldwide who might want to become host centers to provide Montessori training for local communities. These host centers will enhance our presence in their local areas, extending the opportunity for smaller operations to gain access to the best Montessori training and spread the Montessori Method further afield.

MCI is a world leader in providing Montessori training. Modern technology has made this easier, with learner-centered programs delivered through MCI's Virtual Learning Environment. These online programs are in high demand worldwide, boasting proven methods of delivery and assessment. The training enhances teaching expertise, encourages educators to become active collaborators in learning experiences tailored to them personally, and is enabled by dedicated tutor support. Guided by the Montessori approach, this training fosters self-reflection and self-assessment and promotes peer learning. Many of our courses are recognized by NCFE CACHE, a well-regarded UK awarding organization.[34] Our MCI organization works to maintain training that can accommodate the learning requirements of a diverse, worldwide education community audience.

Based in the United Kingdom, we've seen waves of immigration bring families from all across the world to our shores. Our commitment to understanding and respecting these cultures is reflected in the scope of our activities and international partnerships. We share values with entities both at home and abroad, and we cooperate wherever joint activities further the objectives of all involved organizations. As of this writing, Montessori Global Education's footprint includes Albania, Bulgaria, Croatia, Germany, Mexico, Nigeria, Peru, the United Arab Emirates, the United Kingdom, the United States, and Zimbabwe. We're also in discussions or negotiations with organizations in other countries.

All these follow from Dr. Maria Montessori's vision for education, which remains at the core of Montessori Global Education's program: "Early education is the key to the betterment of society."

Home-Start: A Montessori Success Story

When most people think about the United Kingdom, they think about our large cities—London, Manchester, York, or a few others—because that's what they see on TV. What few people realize is that outside those few, large cities, the island of Great Britain is mostly a very rural land, and there's a lot of poverty in our agricultural communities. In

---

[34] Founded in 1981 by combining several organizations providing examinations and certifications to schools and technical colleges, the Northern Council for Further Education became, simply, NCFE, in the 1990s to highlight its increasingly national efforts. The Council for Awards in Care, Health and Education, founded 1945, merged with several similar bodies over the years. The two became NCFE CACHE in 2015.

Conclusion

those, and in towns like them worldwide, unexpected pregnancies are only unexpected by the young women getting pregnant. Some numbers from our most recent census in 2021:

- There were 19.4 million families in the UK.
- Of those, 2.9 million (about 15% of the total) were lone-parent families.
- Of those, 2.5 million (84% of the lone-parent families) were headed by a single mother.
- Only 400,000 families (16%) were headed by single fathers, but that's still a sizable number, and many young fathers struggle equally with their female-led counterparts.[35]

These statistics and many that are similar tell a story of need and of opportunity for Montessori and for similar organizations to get involved and try to address many of these issues. We can offer help and insight, provide opportunities and change lives for the better where we can. I believe that we can do this, and we need to do this because the UK government is not doing it and has not done so for decades.

But there are glimmers of hope. There are some dedicated, committed organizations trying to make a difference.

Home-Start UK is a network, a collective of local, regional community volunteers and expert supporters, trained to help families with young children through their most challenging times. They rely on donations; each local set of volunteers needs support and income from their surrounding communities. Starting in the home, their approach is as

---

[35] Unbylined, "Families and households in the UK: 2022," *Census 2021*. Newport, Wales: Office of National Statistics, 18 May 2023. https://www.ons.gov.uk/peoplepopulationandcommunity/birthsdeathsandmarriages/families/bulletins/familiesandhouseholds/2022, accessed 17 March 2025.

individual as the people they help, and, in my view, this is precisely the type of volunteer network we seek as partners.

With help from Montessori Global, Home-Start West Somerset embarked on a program to reimagine parents as babies' first educators. We put Montessori principles into practice as a guiding framework to support the delivery of this program to families in need. And it worked!

A Closer Look

The seed of an idea was why we chose to partner with Home-Start West Somerset specifically. They come in, assess the needs of families, and set up support pathways, often to help new mothers deal with their needs and the needs of their infants. Home-Start West Somerset, like other Home-Start locations, operates like a franchise in a business landscape. Each office is independent, and they all do their own things based on the needs of that community. In West Somerset, the volunteers were committed and interested community members. (Among those volunteers are other mothers who felt overwhelmed by motherhood at some point.) When we considered our potential involvement, two things made the difference to us:

- The volunteers knew how the patrons felt and could help them from a shared perspective; they were entirely committed to co-creating support, guidance, and solutions with families, for families.

- The willingness of the Home-Start West Somerset team to engage with local people (volunteer network), united as they step up, remain engaged, review and refresh their approaches, and really listen to the needs of their families in all that they do.

That's a winning combination in any project.

Conclusion

One cannot say enough good things about these wonderful people. While some have a job role, part-time and occasional, all staff and volunteers are committed to dedicating their efforts and time to doing something for their community, providing family support. A cause that can make a real, measurable difference to individual lives, and the life chances of babies, children, and young people, especially. This situational landscape led us to believe that our training, all of which are directed at professionals and formal educators, could really make a difference much more broadly.

In 2024, with this team in West Somerset, we piloted our community and volunteer training. It was the first time that our program was offered in this way, but making use of our extensive experience as a teacher-training organization, we developed our delivery model and prepared a model that the team was willing to try. The Montessori Method taught them the pillars of early childhood education. We talked about education in foundational ways, demonstrating how achievable all this stuff was. We connected with everyone, and each person took away a thorough understanding of what "early childhood education" meant and how that could make a difference to the general public. Often, their clients were in very disadvantaged circumstances. Many of these practitioners and their clients had no clue as to what Montessori was, or even that educational philosophies existed. After going through some of our courses, they began to understand Montessori, but we didn't focus on the Method; we focused on preparing them to help their community through a challenging time, supported with an *application* of Montessori in practice.

Think about it this way: Some young mothers were just living hand-to-mouth and, suddenly, they had a baby. What do they do? They came to Home-Start mostly clueless—that's why they came, they didn't have a support system in place. Now, they know and they're able to use that information to champion their babies. "I can do this" is now their mantra.

I have to say, being involved with Home-Start West Somerset has given me a whole new outlook on Montessori's potential. Not only do these children have a better start to life, but, in many cases, the mother has had a restart to her entry into society or her career with an enhanced belief that she's capable of more.

Changing Attitudes

As I have (for lack of a better term) complained throughout this book, Montessori has something of a reputation (deserved in some ways) as an organization in the "elite, out of touch" bracket. Our collaboration with Home-Start is altogether different. It is absolutely in the "very inclusive, accessible" bracket. This has been especially important to Montessori Global because these programs are happening in rural locations, pockets of counties where they don't have a lot of access to things some of us take for granted, and our mandate was crafted to help precisely this type of situation.

Montessori is now being discussed in that environment, and it's had some effects we did not anticipate. One young lady came through the program and took the next step. She had almost nothing when she began—she'd been supported—and wanted to get herself out of this feeling of hopelessness with her baby. Two years later, she is now saying, "I'll now run a group for others in my situation." That's transformational!

Other volunteers, after the baby-start course, set up their own toddler group. It's small, just in their local village hall, but that was inspired by our efforts. They want a Montessori toddler group because they understand enough about the method and want to continue that first effort to the next stage of life. That's groundbreaking! They feel they now understand some sort of parent-educator philosophy that they can carry forward in a new phase of children's lives.

Conclusion

We'll be there, of course, to help people who'd probably never heard the word "pedagogy" but now have one. That could be the beginning of a snowball effect. When others see what they're doing, they may say, "We can do that, too!" And they will.

More centers in rural regions, for hard-to-reach families, can try to give them the insight that Montessori is something they can access and understand; it's not out of their reach. That's what we're packaging.

There's an American acronym, NIMBY, meaning "not in my backyard." Usually, NIMBY means "I don't want a drug treatment center or a sewage plant or some other unpleasant operation in my backyard."

It can, however, also be a denial, "Oh, that's 'not in my backyard'; ours is a good neighborhood." Well, family struggles happen in everyone's backyard, from major metropolises to small villages. In some places, it's the whole town. We tend to forget that because, overall, the UK and the USA are among the richest nations in the world. It's just too easy to forget about such places, especially when everybody actively ignores them. They get no face time on the TV because we don't want to admit such places exist. If no one is advocating for them, it's easy for the government to fail in providing proper, needed services.

In such places, groups like Home-Start have to come in and set up programs to help new families or provide other services based on local needs. And volunteers make it work. We can help train the volunteers, but we need those people to come out of their homes saying, "Here's a need, I want to help." Then, we can say, "We're Montessori, we can help you help others." Once they're trained to facilitate a group and have some experience doing it, they're also trained to run the groups.

We know we can train mothers and fathers, grandmothers and grandfathers, aunts and uncles, caregivers, and many more to operate and lead programs. We're doing that now. We never asked them to "be Montessori." They weren't asked to be training educators, but when we brought that opportunity to them, they asked for more.

We want to access volunteers more directly to say, "You're all valuable. You want professional training, and we have that to offer." So, we get volunteer caregivers, and some have become group facilitators. The group facilitators can become program leaders. And so on.

And, we want more than that. We're now translating much of our support materials for Home-Start into Spanish because our next leap forward is taking this program to Mexico.

Volunteer Prime

In medicine, there's talk of "patient zero"—the first person identified with a disease. That's an ugly term that we want to adapt to be a positive one. In every place, with every Home-Start group or any program like it, we must have a "volunteer prime," that first person who sees a need and says, "I have to do something."

That's the key person. If I had listed these as bullet points, this, for me, is the final bullet. One of the things we've taken away from this partnership is the realization that the capacity for volunteers to inspire other volunteers, and enough bodies to make the program work without burning everybody out. That was not something that we initially recognized or understood. Now that we have some hindsight, going back to our new original mission to get Montessori to everybody wherever it's needed, we need a volunteer prime in every place where it's going to succeed.

Maria Montessori herself was the original volunteer prime. She went into Italian asylums and realized they weren't providing the

Conclusion

services many of those children needed. She made it her mission to change the situation.

This happens all the time in business. An individual sees a need not being met, they have an idea on how to meet that need or, if it is being met, how to meet it better—more efficiently, less expensively, in a new market, whatever problem they see—and they decide to make that solution happen. Sometimes, they don't know how to make it happen, so they say, "I'm going to figure out how to do it or find somebody who can teach me." They learn through a mentor, they experiment, they research, they do what it takes. In Home-Start, that person was Hayley Williams.

Hayley studied early years education, Special Educational Needs and Disabilities (SEND), and family support. She's been part of the early support service in West Somerset for over 15 years, working in the lower super output area of the South West and making positive lasting impacts by empowering families.

Hayley began working for Home-Start in September 2021, after serving as a volunteer since 2012. Presently, Hayley is a family support coordinator for case work referrals in West Somerset, UK. Hayley promotes family activities such as sensory play, encouraging secure parental-child attachments and supporting parents' confidence as their child's first educator. She takes referrals from health workers, educators, early years settings, social care, and self-referral nominees. Hayley supports families along with others in their community—either through groups or with a volunteer initially—and provides a personalized plan of support to meet the challenges they are experiencing, whether that's social, educational, mental, or physical health, rural poverty, or isolation.

What, exactly, is the problem Hayley Williams saw that pushed her to get so involved? She saw that people aren't born knowing how to parent. It doesn't just happen. Those among us who get that instruction get it from our homes and families, somewhat by osmosis. We see what our parents do that works well, and we do the same.

What about those who don't have that example? Hopefully, in the not-so-distant future, there will be many places where those young mothers and fathers can get that coaching from a program like "Baby Start" and many more, inspired-by-Montessori, just like it.

Hayley and those like her deserve recognition. None of them started out to get their faces on the news; many wouldn't want it, but public promotion encourages other people to join the activity. It gives focus and value to the ideals we espouse, which adds to the willingness of governments, private foundations, for-profit businesses, and individuals to provide financial support. It also advertises the program to those who need it, broadening the reach of the program.

Most importantly, it focuses community attention on the need. It's an opportunity to point out, in our case, the need for our youngest children to be in educationally oriented environments. We don't just hope to help our youngest learn in any and every situation; we want them to continue creating such environments for themselves and their children. Among Montessori Global's purposes for existence, we aim to redefine home life as an educational environment.

A Personal Vision

How did Montessori Global become involved in this?

When I had my second child, there was a young woman in the other bed in my hospital room. Truthfully, I don't know that I can honestly call her a "young woman;" she was a girl, probably fresh out of school. The young girl in the bed next to me had the curtain drawn, but I'd seen her go in there. She was tiny and, in the just-over-24 hours that I was in that particular room with my newborn, no one came to see

Conclusion

her. I didn't hear her pick up the phone and talk to someone. As far as I could tell by casual observation, she was all alone.

Was she thrilled to have that baby? She might not have been. She may have decided to give her child a better life through adoption. If that wasn't the case, if she was determined to keep her child, what would've happened to them? Many have heard the statistics; they've been repeated frequently in the press and online:

> Let politicians, schoolteachers and administrators, community leaders, ministers and parents drill into children the message that in a free society, they enter adulthood with three major responsibilities: at least finish high school, get a full-time job and wait until age 21 to get married and have children.
>
> Our research shows that, of American adults who followed these three simple rules, only about 2 percent are in poverty and nearly 75 percent have joined the middle class (defined as earning around $55,000 or more per year). There are surely influences other than these principles at play, but following them guides a young adult away from poverty and toward the middle class.
> —The Brookings Institute[36]

That might be the ideal, but it simply doesn't happen all the time, not yet. That young girl got herself into a situation where she was certainly on her own. No guidance, no apparent family, and, within another 24 hours, she'd probably be out for a taxi ride to who knows where.

---

[36] Ron Haskins, "Three Simple Rules Poor Teens Should Follow to Join the Middle Class," *Brookings.edu*. Washington DC: The Brookings Institution, 13 March 2013. https://www.brookings.edu/articles/three-simple-rules-poor-teens-should-follow-to-join-the-middle-class/, accessed 18 March 2025.

At the beginning of this discussion, I mentioned the needs of our rural population. "Rural" does not always equate to "poverty-stricken," just as "urban" does not always equate to "wealthy." Need knows no boundaries, and our response must be equally universal. Wherever we can help, we need to find those people and do what we can. And, I should add, whoever we are.

I know, absolutely, there are stereotypes that can hinder us and must be overcome. In the first couple of projects I tried to initiate in child-centered practice, I asked, "Get me involved. What can we do to help?" and I was literally met with, "Why you? Why does Montessori think they ought to be involved in this?"

That's not the answer we wanted to hear. We wanted someone to understand that Montessori was created to help in just this situation. This is a strange analogy, but imagine a traveling salesperson with a suitcase full of things. I kind of imagined that they viewed me like one of them. Like they expected me to suddenly produce a suitcase full of beautiful-looking materials, like toys or games or something, I kind of imagined them waiting for me to say, "Maybe you could buy one, just one, for your child." I kind of thought that such a scenario was all they expected from us.

It's extremely disappointing because that isn't even part of my conversation. I'm coming to them with nothing that I want them to buy; that's not what we're here for. After a few such conversations, I started to realize how badly Montessori has been portrayed in the real world. But quite quickly, I started to think—this is our opportunity. We can address this, improve the brand situation, and clarify our messaging. We have value to add, we have support to share, and we have a mission to uphold.

Our first challenge remains overcoming misperceptions and the false ideas surrounding our intentions.

Conclusion

Calls to Action

1. Explore Montessori principles in practice; join us in transforming education.

2. Build confidence in your ability to work with children. Be courageous with your commitment to your chosen pedagogy.

3. Savor learning experiences and opportunities—all of them! Have some #MontessoriMoments.

4. Develop life skills that children need to thrive, now and in the future as adults. To succeed, it's essential that they:
   - Adopt a growth mindset.
   - Take charge of their own learning.
   - Develop curiosity and resilience.
   - Challenge themselves and cultivate a desire to achieve.
   - Find joy in learning experiences.

5. Our experience of learning, exploring, and investigating during the essential birth to age five period shapes lifelong attitudes toward learning. Children must have the space and the freedom to play, explore, go on adventures together, and ignite their imaginations.

An achievable list, I think!

Thank you for taking the time to read our story so far. I encourage you to join us on our path to our next chapter and beyond. Be bold, take charge, and take on the potential in Montessori for you.

#OpportunityEmpowers

Last word

In these times, more than ever before, our hope is that education will offer an aid to better the condition of the world... Our aim is to study the child from this new point of view. With this change in our hearts, we will want to study him in all his different phases, to study all his miracles, to realize how man reaches the stage of man through the child that constructs him... Education is the help we must give to life so that it may develop in the greatness of its powers. To help those great forces which bring the child, inert at birth, to the greatness of the adult being, this should be the plan of education—to see what help we can give.

—Maria Montessori[37]

---

[37] *The 1946 London Lectures, op cit.*

About the Author

Karen Chetwynd – CEO, Montessori Global Education

Karen has worked extensively in the education sector, supporting charitable NGO and commercial success for over 20 years. Consistently focused on achieving high-quality, sustainable outcomes, Karen has worked with a variety of education providers across the UK and internationally, navigating the ever-changing teaching and learning landscape.

Karen holds a Master's in Educational Leadership and Management and is an experienced QAA Reviewer for Higher Education, whilst maintaining an active research interest in authentic assessment practice to benefit learner growth and progression. As a qualified trainer and assessor, Karen has worked in UK Further and Higher Education with a variety of regional and international education providers. With University partners and Ofqual Awarding Organisations, Karen has supported qualifications development from Entry level to Post Graduate, overseeing curriculum design within vocational Teacher Training, Performing Arts and Health, Wellbeing and Fitness specialisms. Karen's work with National Governing Bodies has led to several initiatives focused on supporting access to greater physical education within schools; widening vocational and academic transferability for Performing Arts trainees and helping specialist Higher Education institutions to achieve professional and statutory recognition.

Now, as CEO of Montessori Global Education, a leading learner-centered education organisation, Karen is passionate about setting the tone of Montessori as an accessible, beneficial, and attractive educational pedagogy for everyone, everywhere, able to present learning opportunities that are supportive and nurturing to all our young people.

As a powerful champion for showing how following Montessori principles can expand the thinking capacity of children, Karen advocates for increasing self-confidence, guiding and encouraging learners to enjoy rather than avoid challenges they may face in life.

Karen continues to be hands-on with educational programme delivery and assessment, believing that practical, contemporary experience in industry is essential in understanding learners' needs for today and the future.

BE PART OF SOMETHING BIGGER

Support a vision where every child, everywhere, has access to the power of Montessori education.

Have we inspired you?

Do you want to make a difference?

Join the Momentum in Montessori today!

Scan to discover how you can get involved.

www.montessori-globaleducation.org